T H E
AUTHORITATIVE
WORD

THE AUTHORITATIVE WORD

*Preaching Truth
in a Skeptical Age*

William R.
Bouknight

Abingdon Press / Nashville

THE AUTHORITATIVE WORD:
PREACHING TRUTH IN A SKEPTICAL AGE

Library of Congress Cataloging-in-Publication Data

Bouknight, William R., 1941-
  The authoritative word : preaching truth in a skeptical age / William R. Bouknight.
     p. cm.
  Includes bibliographical references.
  ISBN 0-687-09105-5 (alk. paper)
     1. United Methodist Church (U.S.)—Sermons. 2. Sermons, American—20th century. I. Title.

BX8333.B567 A98 2001
252'.076—dc21

00-048531

01 02 03 04 05 06 07 08 09 10—10 9 8 7 6 5 4 3 2 1

MANUFACTURED IN THE UNITED STATES OF AMERICA

To Gloria Pardee Bouknight—

My wife, best friend,

and the love of my life

CONTENTS

Foreword   9

Introduction   13

1. Worthy Is the Lamb   21

2. God Makes the First Move   27

3. Is Jesus the Only Way to Be Saved?   34

4. The New Birth   40

5. Restoring Bells to Our Steeples   49

6. The Seductiveness of Sodom   57

7. Mary's Revolutionary Song   64

8. The Word of God: Truth Divine   71

9. Jesus Replaced Someone at Calvary   79

10. Jesus and Judgment   86

11. Cleansed by Christ   92

12. The Witness of the Spirit   99

13. If You're a Decent Person, Is That Enough?   105

14. Does Truth Have Many Versions?   112

FOREWORD

Some time ago, I read about a puzzling, somewhat bizarre event that took place in Patterson, California. It not only made the newspapers, it was featured on national television. Fifteen-year-old Felipe Garza, Jr. seemed to be in perfect health, but his girlfriend, Donna Ashlock, had an enlarged heart and needed a transplant.

Felipe told his mother that he was going to die and that he wanted his girlfriend, Donna, to have his heart. Two weeks later, it happened. Felipe died. On the following day, his heart was transplanted to Donna as his last act of love.

Doctors were puzzled. Though apparently outstandingly healthy, Felipe woke up with a pain in the left side of his head, was losing breath, and couldn't walk. His brain died with the bursting of a blood vessel. Though he remained technically alive, the family decided to let the physician remove Felipe's heart for Donna and his kidneys and eyes for others in need of those organs (*The Modesto Bee*, January 6, 1986).

I doubt if doctors ever plumbed the mystery of that death, or if they even tried. We do know the desire for death is powerful. We also know how powerful love is. Those two enormous powers mysteriously came together in Felipe.

Since I read that story, I have thought a lot about Donna, who died three years later. She knew literally what it meant to be alive because of love—the gift of life from another person. I wonder how she talked about that experience.

I don't think I am stretching it to suggest that every Sunday the preacher has as dramatic a story to tell as did Donna. John certainly thought so. He began his first letter with these words:

> That which was from the beginning, which we have heard, which we have seen with our eyes, which we have looked at and our hands have touched—this we proclaim concerning the Word of life. The life appeared; we have seen it and testify to it, and we proclaim to you the eternal life, which was with the Father and has appeared to us. We proclaim to you what we have seen and heard, so that you also may have fellowship with us. And our fellowship is with the Father and with his Son, Jesus Christ. We write this to make our joy complete. (1 John 1:1-4)

John then goes on to talk about the light that illumines our darkness, about the love of Christ on the cross, forgiving us all our sins and cleansing us from all unrighteousness.

Can you think of anything more important than that? We do hold, as Paul said, "this treasure in jars of clay"— nevertheless we hold it—immortal tidings in mortal hands. Of course the transcendent power of it belongs to God, and so "we do not preach ourselves, but Jesus Christ as Lord, and ourselves as your servants for Jesus' sake" (2 Corinthians 4:5). Nevertheless, we preach.

That is the point—the big point—we preach! And that preaching is a kind of heart transplant. Oh, not literally in the fashion of Felipe giving his heart to Donna, but in the sense that is profoundly real: life and light transmitted in the message of preachers, who are "stewards of God's . . . grace" (1 Peter 4:10 RSV).

Bill Bouknight knows and believes this. I have heard him preach. I know what a passionate proclaimer of the gospel he is. His voice, his manner, his identification with his hearers, his timing in storytelling and underscoring a well-crafted statement all combine to make him an effective, hang-on-to-every-word communicator. Thus, I had reservations about how his *written* sermons would "sound." Seldom does the preached word translate effectively into the written word. My reservations are erased. Here are the transforming truths of the gospel plainly and powerfully presented.

I like what Robert Frost said about how poems came to him, because it says so much about preaching. A poem "begins as a lump in the throat, a sense of wrong, a homesickness, a lovesickness. It is never a thought to begin with. . . . It finds the thought and the thought finds the words" (Lawrance Thompson, *Robert Frost: The Years of Triumph 1915–1938*, p. 65). Doesn't that have the feel of John about it? "We declare to you . . . what we have heard, what we have seen with our eyes, what we have looked at and touched with our hands." And doesn't it vibrate with the deep emotion of Paul? "For we do not preach ourselves, but Jesus Christ as Lord." This is all reflected in Bouknight's preaching.

You can't read these sermons without realizing that the writer takes preaching seriously. He knows the place of preaching in the Christian movement. Someone has pointed out that Hinduism lives by ritual and social organization, Buddhism by meditation, and Confucianism by code of manners, but Christianity lives by the "foolishness" of preaching (1 Corinthians 1:21). It is in Christianity that the strange activity of preaching has the core position.

Bill Bouknight gives himself to this strange activity of preaching with discipline and abandon. He comes to the pulpit in humility, knowing that the treasure he is to share is held in a common "jar of clay." But he comes in confidence and conviction because he proclaims not himself but Jesus Christ crucified and risen.

When I read these sermons, I remembered a word from Bishop William A. Quayle written back in 1910 in a book entitled *The Pastor-Preacher*.

> When this preacher comes to a Sunday in his journey through the week, people ask him, "Preacher-man, where were you and what saw you while the workdays were sweating at their toil?" And then of this preacher we may say reverently. "He opened his mouth and taught them, saying:" and there will be another though lesser Sermon on the Mount. And the auditors sit and sob and shout under their breath, and say with their helped hearts, "Preacher, saw you and heard you that? You were well employed. Go out and listen and look another week; but be very sure to come back and tell us what you heard and saw." (*The Pastor-Preacher*, Cincinnati: Jennings & Graham, 1910, p. 310; quoted in *The Manipulator and the Church*, p. 123.)

Bill attempts to listen and look through the ears and eyes of Jesus. He applies Scripture to the critical, personal, and social issues of our time with prophetic and pastoral sensitivity. You will not feel "at ease" reading these sermons; you will be challenged and blessed, for you will hear "the authoritative Word."

Maxie D. Dunnam
President, Asbury Theological Seminary

INTRODUCTION

"Again, if the trumpet does not sound a clear call, who will get ready for battle?" 1 Corinthians 14:8

As a new millennium begins, American mainline Protestantism is in deep trouble. The Presbyterian Church (USA), The United Methodist Church, most branches of the Lutheran Church, the American Baptist churches, the United Church of Christ, the Christian Church (Disciples of Christ), and the Episcopal Church have experienced devastating losses in membership. For example, The United Methodist Church has suffered an average annual net loss of over fifty thousand members for the past thirty-five years. If most mainline Protestant denominations were corporations, their management would have been summarily fired.

Most experts in church history date the beginning of mainline Protestantism's decline at about 1964. However, the virus afflicting the Protestant establishment may have had a much earlier origin. Professor William J. Abraham states that for "two centuries and more many of the intellectual elites . . . have been convinced that the historical faith of the church is untenable."[1]

By the beginning of the nineteenth century, biblical higher criticism was exerting a growing influence in American seminaries. For some professors and students, higher criticism offered fascinating insights into the process by which God inspired people to write down his revealed truth. But for others, the insights of higher criticism displaced the God who inspired the writing of the

Bible. Increasingly, seminary professors began to see the Bible as primarily a human product, an interesting relic of antiquity with limited relevance for a modern era.

A huge question mark was affixed to the Bible in many American seminaries. Many impressionable students came to seminary wanting to acquire tools in order to be more effective in proclaiming the gospel and ministering to people. Many of these students left seminary with a mixture of disillusionment and anger. Much of their zeal for proclaiming God's eternal truth had been stolen from them.

James V. Heidinger II claims that theological liberalism began to move upon the American church scene in the early 1900s. This theological liberalism "tried to excise the supernatural elements out of the biblical text."[2] Once biblical authority had been weakened by higher criticism, the door was open to multiple heresies, all marching under the banner of liberalism.

This liberal "gospel" is strikingly at odds with the good news of the Bible and of orthodox Christianity. If liberalism is embraced, the following are casualties: original sin (because people are basically good); the authority of scripture (because the Bible is just a human document); judgment and hell (because universalism is affirmed); Christ's virgin birth, atonement, deity and resurrection (because Jesus was only a man like other men and did not atone for our sins); and the uniqueness of Christianity (because it is no better than other religions).

H. Richard Niebuhr noted even in the 1950s the pathetic plight of liberalized Protestant churches that took the position that a "God without wrath brought men without sin into a kingdom without judgment through the ministrations of a Christ without a cross."[3] Professor Abraham, a frequent visitor to American mainline churches, points to the "general moral and doctrinal hollowness of the church in its preaching and teaching. . . . More often

than not, one is offered a mixture of thin doctrinal pabu-
lum and moralistic platitude."[4]

Dietrich Bonhoeffer pointed out that a church that
loses its sense of the content of the gospel is much worse
off than a church that goes astray morally. "False doctrine corrupts the life of the Church at its source, and that
is why doctrinal sin is more serious than moral. Those
who rob the Church of the gospel deserve the ultimate
penalty, whereas those who fail in morality have the
gospel there to help them."[5]

Though the contemporary Protestant scene is dismal,
I believe that winds of reformation are blowing, not only
in America but worldwide. When Anglican bishops
gathered at the Lambeth Conference in Canterbury,
England, in the summer of 1998, new waves of conservative theology swept across that denomination, mostly
from Asia, Africa, and South America. This meeting,
held every ten years, attracted over 750 bishops from
around the world. The most controversial item on the
agenda was sex. The conference passed a resolution
upholding "faithfulness in marriage between a man and
a woman in lifelong union," and affirmed abstinence as
"right for those who are not called to marriage."[6] This
resolution, passed by a 526 to 70 vote, was a clear rejec-
tion of the liberal leadership of some American bishops
like John Shelby Spong.

Most observers agree that the General Conference of
The United Methodist Church, which met in Cleveland,
Ohio, in May 2000, turned that denomination sharply in
an evangelical, conservative direction. James M. Wall,
writing in the liberal-leaning *The Christian Century*, con-
cedes that the liberal dominance in United Methodism
has ended.[7]

The recipe for renewal in American Protestantism
begins with repentance. We have treated God's word
with contempt. Rather than regarding it as "a lamp to my

feet and a light for my path" (Psalm 119:105), we have often neglected, belittled, and sometimes despised it.

Following our repentance we must reclaim a high view of Holy Scripture. Methodism's founder, John Wesley, described himself as *homo unius libri,* a man of one book. Like Wesley, we must regard the Bible as the supreme book in our libraries. The Bible, studied intelligently and under the inspiration of the Holy Spirit, must be our true rule for faith and practice. We must regain a sense of awe and wonder in regard to Holy Scripture, believing as did Bishop Mack B. Stokes that "God has taken the initiative to inspire certain people to write down what was on his great heart for his children."[8]

The balance of the prescription for renewal consists of two words: pray and preach. The prophet Jeremiah relayed God's recipe for renewal long ago: "Call to me and I will answer you and tell you great and unsearchable things you do not know" (Jeremiah 33:3). I believe it is no accident that at the beginning of this new millennium, God inspired two American prophets of prayer—Jim Cymbala of Brooklyn and Terry Teykl of Houston—to call the Christian church back to prayer. Teykl reminds us that

> God has placed prayer in the scheme of things in a very unique way. . . . Jesus himself, in addition to teaching often about prayer, modeled it as a radical dependence on the Father for everything. . . . This is by far the healthiest dependency known to mankind. . . . No matter how many resources we own, or how much ability we feel we have, we must continually go before God and ask for His guidance and help. . . . If we will ask Him to awaken our church, He will do it to make a name for His Son.[9]

The miraculous renewal of the Brooklyn Tabernacle is described in Pastor Jim Cymbala's book *Fresh Wind, Fresh Fire.* That pastor and congregation believed fervently that God could renew their church through its Tuesday night prayer meetings. God did![10]

The other key to renewal is preaching. That is the primary focus of this book. I am convinced that the most exciting, transforming truth on earth is the gospel! The orthodox, biblical truths of historic Christianity have not been tried and found wanting. They have been deserted by many fainthearted souls who have been intimidated by a skeptical secular society or a supercilious intellectual elite. This book is one pastor's attempt to articulate biblical, orthodox truth in a relevant fashion.

When I emerged from seminary in 1966, I bore the marks of a liberal theological education. Thankfully, I was anchored to God through a deeply meaningful conversion experience as a teenager. In seminary I was blessed with dedicated scholars who sensitized me to the social dimensions of Christian ethics. Noted Wesleyan scholar Frank Baker and others helped me understand our rich heritage in church history. I had the matchless privilege of studying under that prince of preachers, James S. Stewart, in Edinburgh. But along the way, especially in American seminaries, I ingested some scholarly doubts about the reliability of the Bible. I wondered if I could stand solidly on biblical truth while responding honestly and reasonably to these questions: Why do relatively innocent people suffer? Why did God allow evil to enter this world? Why do evil people seem to prosper? What happens to remote peoples who never hear the gospel? How could a loving God bear to see human beings consigned to an eternal hell?

After about five years in pastoral ministry, helping people wrestle with real-world problems like the death of a child, a betrayal by one's spouse, and the harsh reality of inoperable cancer, I concluded that if the Bible is not my source of authority, then I am left with nothing but opinion. And opinions are like navels. Everybody has one, and all are of dubious value.

In the 1970s, through the loving, prayerful help of

some laypersons, I discovered that the Holy Spirit is a personal, powerful presence who would assist me to the extent that I am open to him. The Holy Spirit confirmed to me the truth of Holy Scripture. I made a solemn commitment to preach biblical, orthodox truth as positively and faithfully as possible. Since that commitment some twenty-five years ago, proclaiming the gospel has been exhilarating! Not that life has been easy. In 1982 our eight-year-old son, Aaron, developed a brain tumor and died. Our hearts were broken. But God kept our spirits secure in him. We learned that the truths we had proclaimed were valid even in the valley of the shadow of death.

I offer the sermons in this volume as a small contribution toward the recovery of biblical, orthodox preaching. I have no illusions that these sermons are better than most. I only know that in preparing and delivering them I sought above all to be faithful to the Bible and orthodox Christian doctrine. "I am not ashamed of the gospel" (Romans 1:16).

Some preachers may be afraid to proclaim a Bible-based, cross-centered gospel for fear of being labeled old-fashioned, simplistic, or naïve. Some are anxious about offending denominational supervisors who are liberal, New Age, or Liberationist in theology. I remind them that the world has always had contempt for the gospel. Paul declared, "For the message of the cross is foolishness to those who are perishing, but to us who are being saved it is the power of God" (1 Corinthians 1:18). He also proclaimed that "we preach Christ crucified: a stumbling block to Jews and foolishness to Gentiles" (1 Corinthians 1:23).

If even 10 percent of a local church will pray fervently and faithfully, and if they will preach and teach the Bible unapologetically and positively, then God will revive that local church and use it as a transforming leaven within its denomination. Lost people will be drawn to such churches because, as Jesus promised, "But I, when I am lifted up from the earth, will draw all men to myself" (John 12:32).

These revived local churches will send laypersons out into the workplace equipped to share the gospel. These renewed, energized churches will challenge all enemies of abundant living—poverty, racism, drugs, alcohol abuse, abortion, and sexual immorality. These Bible-believing, cross-centered churches will be useful for God in reclaiming America. Mainline denominations will start growing again. Mission agencies that have long been bogged down in political and ideological schemes will recover a passion for saving souls.

That is my dream. If this little volume of sermons helps in some small way to articulate the faith in pursuit of that dream, I will rejoice.

How, then, can they call on the one they have not believed in? And how can they believe in the one of whom they have not heard? And how can they hear without someone preaching to them? And how can they preach unless they are sent? As it is written, "How beautiful are the feet of those who bring good news!" (Romans 10:14-15)

NOTES

1. William J. Abraham, *Waking from Doctrinal Amnesia* (Nashville: Abingdon Press, 1995), pp. 22-23.

2. James V. Heidinger II, "The Historicity of Our Faith," *Good News*, May/June 1999, p. 9.

3. H. Richard Niebuhr, *The Kingdom of God in America* (Chicago: Willett, Clark & Company, 1937), p. 193.

4. Abraham, *Waking from Doctrinal Amnesia*, p. 83.

5. Dietrich Bonhoeffer, *The Cost of Discipleship* (London: S.C.M. Press, 1959), p. 264.

6. Diane Knippers, "Anglicans Rumble Over Traditional Morality," *Good News*, November/December 1998, p. 35.

7. James M. Wall, "A simple solution," *The Christian Century*, July 19-26, 2000, p. 739.

8. Mack B. Stokes, *The Bible in the Wesleyan Heritage* (Nashville: Abingdon Press, 1979), p. 16.

9. Terry Teykl, *Pray the Price* (Muncie, Ind.: Prayer Point Press, 1997), pp. 9-11.

10. Jim Cymbala, *Fresh Wind, Fresh Fire* (Grand Rapids, Mich.: Zondervan, 1997).

CHAPTER ONE

WORTHY IS THE LAMB

1 Timothy 2:1-6, Revelation 5:9-10

In 1996 the General Conference of The United Methodist Church was held in Denver. That supreme legislative body of the denomination meets every four years. A Memphis newspaperman, David Waters, noted and reported what may have been the most significant moment in that two-week meeting. The Conference was well into its second day when delegate June Goldman of Iowa got the attention of the presiding bishop. She asked, "Where is the cross?"[1] There was no cross on the platform. Mrs. Goldman felt that a major denomination of the Christian church whose symbol is the cross ought to have a visible cross around. Within the hour, a large cross was placed on the stage. Perhaps June Goldman was a prophet sent from God to pose God's question to these United Methodists: *Where is the cross? Have you forgotten it? Would you be willing to restore it to center stage in your hearts and on your agendas?*

The devil won't mind too much if the church does nothing more than teach the golden rule. The devil won't get upset if we just read theological books, especially those that disagree with the Bible. The devil has no real problem if the church feeds the hungry, as long as we never mention Jesus. But it drives him crazy for us to talk about Jesus Christ, God's Son, dying on a cross for the sins of humanity.

In our secular society, many people either ridicule the

cross or ignore it. Long ago, Paul said that non-Jews regarded the message of the cross as foolishness (1 Corinthians 1:23). Many still do. A prominent New York City seminary professor, in a speech before a large interdenominational assembly, declared, "We don't need to hear about somebody hanging on a cross, and blood dripping, and all that stuff." Most of the audience responded with a standing ovation.

Other people treat the cross as nothing more than an ornament for the necklace, ear, or some other part of the anatomy. When a jewelry store clerk was asked by a customer for a cross, she asked, "Do you want a plain one or one with the little man on it?"

The message of the cross is the heartbeat of our faith. Most mainline denominations have in their creeds or confessions of faith a high theology of the cross. Fairly typical is this affirmation in the United Methodist *Book of Discipline:* "The offering of Christ, once made, is that perfect redemption, propitiation, and satisfaction for all the sins of the whole world, both original and actual, and there is none other satisfaction for sin but that alone" (Article 20). Even more important, the Bible declares, "For Christ died for sins once for all, the righteous for the unrighteous, to bring you to God" (1 Peter 3:18). Here are two great biblical affirmations concerning the cross.

Salvation Is Available to All

God desires that everyone experience salvation—even convicted murderers on death row. Verse 4 in our Timothy text tells us that God "wants all men to be saved and to come to a knowledge of the truth."

What is salvation? It means that my sin is forgiven; that the disease of sin working in me is brought under control; and that I am restored to right relationship with

God, myself, and other people. My eternal reservations in heaven are confirmed. I am filled with the Holy Spirit and changed into a useful instrument for God. Salvation includes all of that.

At my church in Memphis we have a service on Saturday evenings called "Saturday Night Alive." It is thoroughly contemporary. Everybody, including the preacher, dresses informally. A band with wonderful singers and musicians leads the music. People don't mind lifting their hands and swaying when they sing. They help me preach by saying an occasional "yes" or "amen." It's a lively place. Half the folks who attend are unchurched.

One Saturday night recently I looked out and saw my friend Carolyn McKenzie in the audience. Carolyn is a former Army nurse who served in Vietnam. She is a dedicated Christian who is on a mission. She rescues victims from the sexually oriented businesses of Memphis. Young women get trapped in those places, making $500 a night but becoming dependent on drugs in order to tolerate the work. Carolyn and some friends in our church and other churches liberate these women, finding them places to live, new jobs, transportation, and self-respect. One particular Saturday night, I saw Carolyn sitting there. With her were two young women whom she had recently liberated from the clubs. I thanked God that our church doors are wide enough to allow these young women to enter and feel comfortable with the rest of us sinners.

Wouldn't it be wonderful if all of our churches could triple their number of recovery groups—Alcoholics Anonymous, Narcotics Anonymous, grief recovery, recovery from abuse, and all other groups that use the twelve-step path from brokenness to wholeness. Jesus said, "It is not the healthy who need a doctor, but the sick" (Matthew 9:12). All of us suffer from a sickness that only the cross can cure.

Just imagine if even 5 percent of the membership of historically white churches were African American and vice versa. Think how this could expand their outreach and ministry. Do you think for one moment that the relevance of the gospel depends on skin pigmentation? Of course not. Don't you think that Jesus would be pleased if homosexual persons felt sure that they would be welcome in our churches? No, the Bible does not approve of their lifestyle. But there are things in my lifestyle and yours of which the Bible doesn't approve; and yet the church has welcomed us. You know, God cleans his fish after he catches them.

We don't have to compromise the gospel or the Bible in order to open wide the doors of the church. The doors of the church must be as open as the arms of the Master.

Salvation Was Purchased by the Blood of Jesus Christ, the Lamb of God

In Revelation 5:9 we read that "you [the Lamb] were slain, and with your blood you purchased men for God from every tribe and language and people and nation."

Throughout Old Testament times, lambs were offered as sacrifices for sin. Jesus came as the perfect Lamb of God whose death on the cross became the all-sufficient sacrifice for all time and all believers. When John the Baptist saw Jesus coming to him at the Jordan River, John said, "Look, the Lamb of God, who takes away the sin of the world!" (John 1:29).

Methodist founder John Wesley confided to his friend Charles Perronet in late-1774, "If we could once bring all our preachers, itinerant and local, uniformly and steadily to insist on those two points, 'Christ dying for us' and 'Christ reigning in us,' we should shake the trembling gates of hell."[2]

Isn't it ironic that the first cloned animal was a lamb? The possibility has been raised that we could produce countless carbon copies of that lamb. Yet Jesus, the Lamb of God, declares that each one of us is gloriously different! So important to God is each of us that Jesus would have been sacrificed for even one of us.

Jesus Christ, the Lamb of God, has been sacrificed for our sin. If we repent and trust in him as Savior and Lord, all of our sin is washed away. The living Christ-Spirit saturates and transforms us. Our places in heaven are reserved and guaranteed.

But, you might ask, how did the death of Jesus Christ atone for the sins of the world? I would respond this way. On Calvary's cross, a great supernatural deed was done; but I'm afraid to trust my little mind and limited vocabulary to describe the mystery. The cross is vastly bigger than our ideas about it. It's not important that I get my mind around it as long as I can get my heart around it. Even though I don't comprehend the cross completely, I have been saved by it.

There is only one way to bypass judgment and to be sure of spending eternity in heaven. There is only one way to bring the disease of sin under control and to experience a life of fulfillment and joy. That way is to repent and believe the good news that "God so loved the world that he gave his one and only Son, that whoever believes in him shall not perish but have eternal life" (John 3:16).

The Lamb of God was offered on Calvary's cross so that we could be saved and transformed through the grace of God. That grace is yours if you simply say sincerely, "I am a sinner for whom Jesus died. I claim him by faith as Savior and Lord."

NOTES

1. David Waters, "12 Words Refocus Methodist Meeting," *The Commercial Appeal*, April 29, 1996.

2. John Wesley, *The Letters of the Rev. John Wesley, A.M. Vol. VI.* ed. by John Telford, B.A. (London: The Epworth Press, 1931), p. 134.

CHAPTER TWO

GOD MAKES THE FIRST MOVE

John 6:44

As I strolled the beautiful Augusta National Golf Course on a glorious April day, I noticed the famous German golfer Bernhard Langer practicing for the Masters Tournament. He is a two-time winner of that prestigious event. As I watched him, I thought about his personal testimony. Langer says that when he won the Masters in 1985, his priorities were golf, golf, and more golf; then himself; then a little time with his wife; and occasionally a nod toward God. He says that if his golf was not going well, his entire life was miserable.

Then in 1985, one week after he won the Masters, he was invited by a friend to attend the Tour Bible Study led by Larry Moody. For some reason, he decided to go. There he learned for the first time that he needed to be reborn in order to have abundant and eternal life. Within a matter of a few months, he and his wife, Vikki, had received Christ as their Savior and Lord.

Notice that I said that Bernhard Langer agreed to attend that Tour Bible Study *for some reason.* I think I know the reason. Christians of the Wesleyan tradition call it "prevenient grace." That is a term describing God's first attempts to reach us, to call us, and to save us. God always makes the first move toward us. The word "prevenient" is a combination of two Latin root words: *pre* meaning "before" and *venire* meaning "to come." "Prevenient" means that which comes first or in advance. Grace simply means undeserved love, that unmerited favor which God always feels toward us. So prevenient grace is that first loving move God makes in our direction.

Prevenient grace is that first slight twinge of conscience, that vague discontent with one's godless condition, that first slight interest in spiritual matters. Picture yourself asleep in a boat. The boat is drifting down a river, moving closer and closer to a dangerous waterfall. The water makes considerable noise, screening out other sounds. But someone on the shore is shouting your name. Prevenient grace is God calling your name over the noise of a sinful, distracting world.

Jesus said, "No one can come to me unless the Father who sent me draws him, and I will raise him up at the last day" (John 6:44). I invite the Holy Spirit to teach us at least four truths from this mighty verse.

We Are Utterly Lost in Our Natural State

Note the first part of that verse: "No one can come to me unless the Father . . . draws him." In other words, without the grace of God, we would feel no need whatsoever for God, no perception of sin, no desire to live righteously.

Consider certain big-name sports heroes in professional football and basketball who have gotten into big trouble, primarily because of drugs. Most of us read about these tragedies in the newspaper and we wonder why the guy would be so stupid. He has money, fame, and an adoring public. He has the American dream. Why would he risk it all for an illegal drug?

But consider this—until that sports hero has responded to the grace of God, he has no peace or joy in his soul. Though he has the American dream, it almost mocks him, saying: "Ha! Look at all you've got, but you're still not really content." So the temptation to abuse drugs is even more powerful for him. He wants above all else to feel "high"—and if he can't find a natural high, he will settle for a chemical version.

Paul, in his Letter to the Romans, quotes from Psalms and Isaiah as he describes the condition of people before they respond to the grace of God in Christ.

> "There is no one righteous, not even one; there is no one who understands, no one who seeks God. All have turned away, they have together become worthless; there is no one who does good, not even one. . . . ruin and misery mark their ways, and the way of peace they do not know. There is no fear of God before their eyes." (Romans 3:10-12, 16-18)

That is the condition of people before they respond to God's first overtures.

God Draws Us to Himself

"No one can come to me unless the Father who sent me draws him, and I will raise him up at the last day," John 6:44 tells us. Our God is a searching, drawing, attracting God. He searches for everybody. In Ezekiel 34:11, God says, "I myself will search for my sheep."

Francis Thompson referred to God as "the hound of heaven," pursuing us as persistently as a hound tracks a deer. In Luke 15:4, Jesus said, "Suppose one of you has a hundred sheep and loses one of them. Does he not leave the ninety-nine in the open country and go after the lost sheep until he finds it?"

That's the character of God—always seeking the sheep that is lost. Referring to himself, Jesus said, "For the Son of Man came to seek and to save what was lost" (Luke 19:10).

If you attended church last Sunday, are you sure you know why? It would be interesting to give all worshipers a dose of truth serum and then have them write down an absolutely honest answer. Some would say, "My wife is obviously disappointed when I skip church, so, I go to please her." Some would say, "I have this friend at work who attends a church of another denomination. Every Monday morning he asks me if I went to church on Sunday. When I tell him I didn't make it, he regards me as a heathen. So I go to keep him from feeling so spiritually superior."

Tommy Lasorda, former manager of the Los Angeles Dodgers, tells about an experience he had in church. One Sunday he was in Cincinnati for a ball game against the Reds. That morning he went to early morning Mass and happened to see the Reds' manager there. They were old friends and sat beside each other during Mass. Afterward, the Reds' manager said, "Tommy, I'll see you at the ballpark. I'm going to hang around a little." Lasorda said that when he reached the door, he glanced back over his shoulder. He noticed that his friend was praying at the altar and lighting a candle. He said, "I thought about that for a few moments. Then, since we needed a win very badly, I doubled back and blew out his candle."

Isn't it strange how we often don't want anybody to get ahead of us spiritually?

Though we are drawn to God and church by a variety of motives, the foremost attraction is grace. We are responding to God's grace. For some of us, it's prevenient grace, the first dawning of God's grace. Others responded to prevenient grace years ago; now they are responding to subsequent installments of grace. But some expression of God's grace beckons us to worship; I am convinced of that.

The first meaningful commitment I made to Christ was in a little country church in upstate South Carolina. My father was the pastor. A revival was held in the spring of the year when I was twelve years old. A young college student, Phil Jones, on his way toward ordained ministry, was the guest preacher. I look back and wonder why I agreed to go with Papa to that revival meeting. He never required me to attend church except on Sunday mornings. I'm sure I had homework to do that evening. There were television programs—not many, but a few, like *The Lone Ranger*. But something pulled me to go with Papa that evening. What was it? I think it was God through his prevenient grace.

Prevenient grace caused a Jewish ruler named Nicodemus to seek out Jesus for a private conference one night. Prevenient grace caused a tax collector named Zacchaeus to climb a sycamore tree so he could see Jesus. Prevenient grace prepared a man named Saul of Tarsus to encounter Jesus on the road to Damascus, and there he became Paul the Apostle.

I have had so many young adults come to me over the years relating a similar story that I refer to it as the young-adult syndrome. Here is the typical way the male version sounds:

> I grew up around the church, but as I got older, I got away from it. At college I almost forgot about God entirely; oh, maybe at Easter or Christmas, I would drop by the church to please my folks, but it didn't mean anything. I tried everything the world told me would make life really good. I had multiple sex partners. I smoked pot. I drank enough booze to float a boat. But I still wasn't satisfied inside; in fact, these excursions into the fast lane, while exhilarating for the moment, made me feel worse.
>
> After I got out of college I worked hard to make some serious money, and I did. I bought a red sports car. Now the girls really noticed me. Then I fell deeply in love with someone and she loved me too. On our wedding day, I said to myself, "This is what I have been missing all this time. Finally, this will enable me to be totally satisfied." But as wonderful as our love was and is, there was still something unsatisfied inside of me.

Then our first child came along, and that was fantastic! What a feeling it was to hold something that precious in my arms for the first time! I was overcome with joy; but I still had an unsatisfied feeling in my heart.

Finally, my wife and I had some long talks about this feeling. She felt the same thing. We concluded that perhaps we have a spiritual part of us inside—sort of like an invisible organ in the body—that must be nourished, or we will never be satisfied. That's when we headed to church. It seemed strange at first, but it wasn't long before we knew that this spiritual part of us was being nourished. We found what we had been longing for and missing.

I have heard versions of that story countless times. Who do you think creates that unsatisfied feeling inside when we are apart from him? God is at work through prevenient grace.

Something Inside Us Resists God's Call

The Greek verb in John 6:44—to draw—is a strange word. It implies resistance. It is not an easy pulling but one that has opposition. It is the word you use for pulling or drawing a heavily loaded net up on a beach. It is like reeling in an artificial lure with a big bass on the other end. There is resistance.

While God is drawing us to himself through prevenient grace, the enemy—the evil one—creates all kinds of resistance. The evil one whispers: "If you get mixed up with Jesus, you'll have to quit everything that's fun. You will lose some of your best buddies. He might interfere with your hunting and fishing. He might turn you into some kind of hypocrite. He might get into your bank account. You might become a wimp."

The resistance will be there. Just count on it. The evil one will not surrender any of us without a fight. But also remember that "the one who is in you is greater than the one who is in the world" (1 John 4:4).

If You Respond to Prevenient Grace, You Are on Your Way to Salvation

There are further stages of grace up ahead. If you compare God's grace to the rooms in a house, prevenient grace is just a gentle nudge toward the front porch. That front porch is called repentance. When one enters the front door, one becomes a believer or a Christian. Notice Jesus' promise in John 6:44: those who respond with faith to God's drawing will find that at the end of their lives or at the end of history (whichever comes first), Jesus will raise them up to eternal life. Have you felt God's grace pulling you to him? Have you responded? Are you responding?

A former colleague of mine at Christ Church in Memphis, the Reverend Gene Barnes, told me a story about the great composer Alexander Borodin. Mr. Borodin had a little granddaughter who was a great favorite of his. One day he lifted her up on a piano bench and invited her to play a duet with him. Using two fingers she pecked out the familiar "Chopsticks" while Mr. Borodin improvised an accompaniment. She was absolutely delighted. So her proud grandfather set it down on paper. A friend, Franz Liszt, added variations and adapted this piece for a full orchestra. It was later played and recorded by the Columbia Symphony Orchestra. When Borodin played a recording of this piece for his granddaughter, she said in great awe, "Was that me?"

If any of us plays God's song, it will be because God in his grace beckoned us to the piano bench, put our fingers on the right keys, and taught us his melody. How wonderful is the grace of God!

CHAPTER THREE

IS JESUS THE ONLY WAY TO BE SAVED?

Matthew 22:1-14, John 14:5-6

It may surprise you to know what many Americans consider to be the only serious sin. No, not murder. Even murder has its mitigating factors. A recent article in *Christianity Today* declares that many Americans consider the worst sin to be intolerance. And guess who are the worst sinners in the minds of many Americans: evangelical Christians. One writer said that Christians are seen as the pit bulls of culture wars—small brains, big teeth, strong jaws, and no interest in compromise.

A guest on National Public Radio shocked even his liberal host when he objected to the Southern Baptist belief that a lot of people are going to hell. By the way, that's not just a Southern Baptist belief; that's a biblical truth. The guest on National Public Radio said that the evaporation of four million Baptists who believe that garbage would leave the world a better place. Sounds to me like that guest was willing to tolerate everybody except the Baptists. Are the Baptists really that hard to tolerate? Some of my best friends are Baptists.

Dr. Laura Schlessinger, the popular and controversial radio host, has remarked on the large volume of hate mail she receives for believing in moral absolutes. Her enemies ask her to be more tolerant of other moral views, but they don't want to tolerate Dr. Laura's views. Too much of what passes as tolerance in America is just moral indifference. Too many Americans regard truth as merely opinion. In their view, goodness is only what the majority says it is.

Jesus said many politically incorrect things, but the most shocking is recorded in John 14:6: "I am the way and the truth and the life. No one comes to the Father except through me." Later, Peter made that claim even more blatantly. Referring to Jesus, he said in Acts 4:12, "Salvation is found in no one else, for there is no other name under heaven given to men by which we must be saved."

Now, just a brief explanation about the word "salvation." That word is used in a variety of ways throughout scripture. It is a term that describes rescue from any kind of calamity. It can be used to refer to victory in battle or recovery from a disease. But the Bible also teaches about ultimate or eternal salvation. To be defeated in battle or to lose one's health is not the ultimate calamity. The ultimate calamity is to face a holy and righteous God on the Day of Judgment without a Savior.

Many Americans are spiritual seekers. They aren't yet committed to a higher power, but they are spiritually hungry and searching for solid sustenance. Something in them is rankled by this idea of Jesus being the only way to salvation. But when Jesus said these words, he was motivated not by arrogance but by compassion. If you will suspend judgment for just a little while, and consider with me a simple story Jesus told, I believe that Jesus' claim will begin to make sense.

In Matthew 22, Jesus told a story about a king whose son was getting married. Undoubtedly the king rented the banquet hall and ballroom of a big hotel and threw a bodacious bash. Remember, in first-century Palestine, most people were poor. But even among the poor, a wedding called for a weeklong party. This was the one occasion in life when the poor splurged, even if on borrowed funds. So if the king with all his resources was throwing a party, it was probably going to be a Middle Eastern version of Mardi Gras.

It's interesting that Jesus would compare the kingdom of God to the biggest party anyone could imagine. He was saying that the dominant mood in the kingdom of God is joy. And you would assume that everybody would want to come. Wrong! Many specially invited guests refused to come.

Jesus was clearly referring to the Jewish people, who had been invited to be God's chosen people. They were to be his cradle for the Messiah, a chosen race and a holy priesthood, designed to bless the entire world. But the Jews persecuted most of the prophets sent by God, and tragically, they rejected the Messiah when he came. Verse 7 indicates that God would judge the Jews severely for having rejected his messengers and his invitation. Verses 8 through 10 tell us that the king then extended his invitation to everybody, the good and the bad, the rich and the poor. It is a glorious truth that every person is invited into the kingdom of God. Come as you are! It is assumed that once you experience the kindness of the king, you will want nothing more than to act according to his will.

Then comes that difficult final part of the story, verses 11 through 14. The king found a fellow at the party who was not wearing the proper attire and kicked him out. You probably are thinking: if the king is tolerant enough to let anyone come to his party, why should he get bent out of shape over what he or she is wearing?

Augustine, a great church leader of the fourth century, has helped us on this point. He explained that each person who accepted the king's invitation was given proper attire for the banquet. The king was aware that poor people would not have proper clothing for such an occasion. He did not want anyone to feel inferior. So the king provided the right clothes to wear.

But this fellow in verse 11 was a rebel at heart. He disregarded the generosity of the king and decided to come on his own terms. Augustine believed that Jesus in this story was connecting the wedding garment to the "robe of righteousness" that Isaiah the prophet talked about (Isaiah 61:10). God's gift of salvation is that robe of righteousness, that proper wedding garment. If you are not humble enough to know you need it, if you are not grateful enough to accept it, you cannot come to God's party.

The only person who cannot experience God's forgiveness is the one who thinks he or she has no sin. The only person who cannot be saved is that one who sees no need for the cross of Christ. Jesus does not exclude us. He offers—free of charge—one path to salvation, but many reject this offer. They exclude themselves.

Some people believe that all religions are basically the same; it doesn't matter which one you follow, as long as it works for you. Supposedly, all spiritual paths lead up the same mountain. While it is true that there is some common ground shared by the world's religions, there are significant differences. Jesus boldly put Christianity in a class by itself when he said that the only path to God is through himself.

Lee Strobel, that gifted teacher and preacher at Saddleback Church, has pointed out that every other religion but Christianity is based on people doing something to somehow earn favor with God. Some say you have to use a Tibetan prayer wheel, give money to the poor, avoid eating certain foods, pray in a certain direction, or go through a cycle of reincarnations. These are all attempts to earn enough favor with God to deserve his salvation.

Other religions are spelled "D-O" because they teach

that people must do a variety of religious rituals to work their way to God. But Christianity is not spelled "D-O." Christianity is spelled "D-O-N-E." On the cross, Jesus Christ has done what was needed. He paid our penalty. When we accept him as personal savior and leader, we are endorsing that transaction by faith. We are donning our wedding garment and are ready for God's party.

Jesus, in Matthew 7:13-14, said, "Enter through the narrow gate. For wide is the gate and broad is the road that leads to destruction, and many enter through it. But small is the gate and narrow the road that leads to life, and only a few find it." What is the small gate and narrow road? It is the way of the humble penitent who declares to Jesus, "I am a sinner who cannot fix my sin problem. But I believe you offered the only cure when you died for me on the cross. I accept it gladly, and in gratitude I invite you to be the leader of my life."

I would not dare to tell a Muslim or Jew that he or she is bound for hell. Only God can make that judgment. But neither am I authorized by the Bible to tell someone that as long as he is sincere and faithful in any religion, he will end up in heaven. Jesus said, "I am the way and the truth and the life," not "a way, a truth, and a life." He said, "No one comes to the Father but by me." Therefore, if I have an opportunity to share the gospel with a Jew or Muslim, I will jump at the chance. I will not approach him or her in a condescending or threatening way, but, in the words of D. T. Niles, as "one beggar telling another beggar where to find food."[1]

Lee Strobel tells about some friends who had a baby girl who developed jaundice—a disorder of the liver that caused her skin and the whites of her eyes to turn yellow. It is a fairly common problem for newborns. Their pediatrician told them that this is potentially a devastating disease, but that fortunately it is easily cured. He explained that by placing the baby under a special light, the liver would be stimulated to begin working normally. The light would cure their daughter. But let's suppose that the parents had said, "That prescription sounds too easy. Put her under a light? We have a better idea. We will scrub her with soap and water, and dip her in some bleach instead. Certainly if we work hard enough to scrub her that way, we could get her normal coloring back." The doctor would have looked at them and said, "No, you don't understand. There is only one way to cure your daughter." The parents could have said, "But Doc, there are many medical theories circulating concerning the treatment of various diseases. You say that the light treatment is the only way, but aren't you being a bit narrow-minded?" The doctor might have turned red in the face and said, "You hardheaded, stubborn parents! You're going to jeopardize the life of your child if you don't follow my instructions. There is only one cure for her. Now that is the truth!"

Every person has a terminal illness called sin. The reason that followers of Jesus cling to him so tightly is that he is the only cure. When Jesus said, "I am the way and the truth and the life," he was being no more arrogant than a physician who says there is only one cure for a jaundiced infant.

"For God so loved the world that he gave"—not many ways but one way—"his one and only Son, that whoever believes in him shall not perish but have eternal life" (John 3:16).

NOTE

1. Quoted in James C. Logan, ed., *Theology and Evangelism in the Wesleyan Heritage* (Nashville: Kingswood Books, 1994), p. 136.

CHAPTER FOUR

THE NEW BIRTH

John 3:1-8

When Jimmy Carter was President, the press often described him as a "born-again Southern Baptist." Everybody knew what a Southern Baptist was (just a Methodist unafraid of water and willing to tithe). But the term "born again" was a mystery to many.

There was always something different about Jimmy Carter. Even his political enemies detected in him an inner peace, a spiritual depth, and a transcendent commitment. Perhaps Jimmy Carter's differentness had to do with this business of being born again. Let's explore it.

There would be no Methodist Church today were it not for the doctrine of new birth. John Wesley's personal experience of it launched the Methodist movement. In January 1738, John Wesley was returning to England from a less than successful missionary journey to Georgia. His deep anxieties were reflected in his diary: "I went to America to convert the Indians; but Oh! who shall convert me? Who, what is he that will deliver me from this evil heart of unbelief? I have a fair summer religion. I can talk well . . . but let death look me in the face, and my spirit is troubled."[1]

Four months later, on May 24, 1738, John Wesley went "very unwillingly" to a prayer meeting on Aldersgate Street in London. The following day he recorded the experience in his diary: "About a quarter before nine, while he [a layman reading Martin Luther's preface to the Epistle to the Romans] was describing the change which God works in the heart through faith in Christ, I felt my heart strangely warmed. I felt I did trust in Christ, Christ alone, for salvation, and an assurance was given me that he had taken away *my* sins, even *mine*, and saved *me* from the law of sin and death."[2]

Methodism was born when John Wesley was newly born in the Spirit as his heart was strangely warmed. The United Methodist Church and most mainline churches are true to their purpose and charter only when they are calling people to experience the heart-warming, life-changing, soul-saving experience of new birth.

The doctrine of new birth comes from an experience Jesus had with a rich Jewish ruler named Nicodemus. The account of their conversation as given in John 3 is the most highly developed dialogue in all the Gospels between Jesus and a named individual. How strange it is that a member of "Who's Who in Jerusalem" would seek out Jesus, a rustic, radical, itinerant preacher. Jesus was usually surrounded by ordinary folks, but here we see him with a real aristocrat.

Nicodemus arranged to meet Jesus at night because he wanted the meeting to be secret and off the record. After all, it would have been politically damaging for Nicodemus to be seen with Jesus in broad daylight. It would be akin to the Democratic nominee for president seeking counsel from the leader of the Christian Coalition: while it might do him good personally, it would not help him politically.

Nicodemus respectfully called Jesus "Rabbi" and sought to compliment him. But Jesus quickly cut to the core issue. He said that "no one can see the kingdom of God unless he is born again." "How can a man be born when he is old?" Nicodemus asked. "Surely he cannot enter a second time into his mother's womb to be born!"

Here was a classic miscommunication. Nicodemus was thinking in physical terms, while Jesus was declaring spiritual truth.

Speaking of miscommunication, I am reminded of a man named Don who attended a business convention in Miami Beach. Because his duties as a convention leader were heavy, he was so busy that he failed to telephone his wife back in Illinois. Finally, after three days away from home, he managed to send a quick e-mail message to his wife. Because he typed it hurriedly, he made just a small mistake. He left one letter off of one word. The message his wife received was this: "Dear Honey: I am being kept quite busy at the convention so this message must be brief. I'm having a wonderful time. Wish you were her. Love, Don."

When Don returned home, he had a considerable miscommunication to explain. Nicodemus and Jesus started off with that level of miscommunication. In order to unpack the scriptural truth of new birth, let's ask and answer three questions.

What Is New Birth?

John Wesley described new birth as the

> great change which God works in the soul when he brings it into life: when he raises it from the death of sin to the life of righteousness. It is the change wrought in the whole soul by the almighty Spirit of God when it is "created anew in Christ Jesus", when it is "renewed after the image of God", "in righteousness and true holiness", when the love of the world is changed into the love of God, pride into humility, passion into meekness; hatred, envy, malice, into a sincere, tender, disinterested love for all mankind.[3]

The experience of new birth can be emotional or calm.

New birth is not something we do. It is an act of God that often follows our decision to repent and trust in Jesus Christ as Savior and Lord. New birth is the first part of the process called conversion. Wesley taught that this supernatural change is so vital that spiritual life itself "commences when we are born again."[4]

My friend Erv Ethell is a retired Air Force officer, a World War II fighter pilot. If you ask how he is doing, he always replies, "I'm clear-headed, blue-eyed and unafraid." In a recent note he offered this testimony: "Next Easter Sunday will be my fifth anniversary of being a born-again Christian. I'll never forget the great feeling and peace of mind. The sermon of that day put God's arrow through my heart."

But you see, that sermon did not cause his new birth. Nor was it caused by his repentance and belief in Christ, though those factors placed him where God could reach him. God alone caused new birth in my friend.

New birth is a recurring theme of scripture. Peter in his Epistle speaks of being "born again, not of perishable seed, but of imperishable" (1 Peter 1:23). James writes about God begetting us with "the word of truth" (James 1:18). And Paul declares that "if anyone is in Christ, he is a new creation" (2 Corinthians 5:17).

How do you know if you have experienced new birth? You will be able to say a firm "yes" to the following statement: "Through Jesus Christ, God has fundamentally changed my life."

Is the Experience of New Birth
Necessary for Everybody?

Absolutely yes, said Jesus: "No one can see the kingdom of God unless he is born again" (John 3:3). When God created the first human beings, they were righteous and holy. But they were equipped with the dangerous capacity for free will. In response to temptation, Adam and Eve forfeited their intimate relationship with God. They became unholy and unhappy. Death entered the world, not just physical death but also spiritual death. Human beings came under the operational control of the evil one.

All descendants of Adam and Eve became like computers with faulty software. They can't work right because they are miswired. They cannot fix their own problem. God is the only spiritual computer specialist who can fix it. It cost him a cross in order to be able to do it. One of the awful failings of many mainline churches in America is that they no longer preach that it is necessary to be born again. They imply that a person can be saved by just hanging around the church. But hanging around the church no more makes you a Christian than hanging around Beale Street in Memphis makes you a musician.

In John 8:31-41, Jesus warned the Jews that they should not feel spiritually secure just because Abraham was their ancestor. Neither will it help a person one iota on the Day of Judgment to be able to say, "I was a member of the United Methodist or Presbyterian or Lutheran Church," if he or she cannot also declare, "Through Jesus Christ, God has fundamentally changed my life."

The dangerous message that some preachers disseminate is that we're all okay. They imply that if you were baptized as a baby, that if you try to keep the Ten Commandments and are fairly respectable, and that if you attend church and contribute a little money, then you have satisfied God's requirements. That is a damnable lie.

John Wesley, Methodism's founder, was concerned about the false security of works-righteousness. He declared:

Go to church twice a day, go to the Lord's table every week, say ever so many prayers in private; hear ever so many sermons, good sermons, excellent sermons, the best that ever were preached; read ever so many good books—still you must be born again. . . . Let this, therefore, if you have not already experienced this inward work of God, be your continual prayer, "Lord, add this to all thy blessings: let me be 'born again.' "[5]

Woe to us preachers if we send the message that as long as you read the scriptures occasionally, pray, and serve on some church committee, you'll slide into heaven.

You must be born again. I must be born again. Billy Graham and the Pope must be born again. You cannot be happy or holy unless you have been born again. Can you honestly say, "Through Jesus Christ, God has fundamentally changed my life"?

How Can I Make the New Birth Happen?

The answer is simple: We can't. Nicodemus would have been so pleased if Jesus had given him a spiritual self-help formula to bring about new birth, such as fast three days a week, pray ten times a day, and give away 20 percent of one's income instead of 10 percent.

We Americans would like that, except for that 20 percent levy on our incomes. We usually believe that anything worth having can either be bought or earned. But you can't purchase a "do-it-yourself" salvation kit for $19.99. Neither can you obtain a certificate of salvation by working on three low-income houses and putting in a hundred hours of community service fighting racism, sexism, and poverty.

Jesus taught that the Holy Spirit is the obstetrician of new births. And the Holy Spirit is like the wind. It blows where it will. No human being can control the Holy

Spirit any more than he or she can direct the wind. There is a sovereign spontaneity about it. While none of us can orchestrate the new birth, we can place ourselves in a favorable position to be reached by the Holy Spirit.

That makes sense. If you are looking for a racehorse, you go to Kentucky. If golf is your passion, you go to Myrtle Beach. If you want to make it big in country music, you go to Nashville. Similarly, if you want to encounter God, it helps to place yourself where God can reach you easily. When we are faithful in worship, when we read our Bibles and pray, and when we fellowship with born-again Christians, we place ourselves in a favorable environment for the miracle of new birth. Just remember where John Wesley was when it happened to him: in a Bible study group on Aldersgate Street in London.

Sometime in the early 1980s I heard a layperson from Christ United Methodist Church, Memphis, give his testimony at Lake Junaluska, North Carolina. I never imagined that I would one day be that man's pastor. Dr. Tom Shipmon's testimony was powerful and unforgettable. Tom said that as a young adult, he was a complacent churchgoer. He was vocationally successful as a dental surgeon. He made lots of money, and gave liberally to the church. He was elected to numerous leadership positions in the church. But he did not have a personal relationship with God.

Tom said that he tried hard to buy happiness. He spent every Tuesday at the country club, playing golf and drinking. He was almost always late for dinner at home. He recalls that in one year he bought four different cars. But they made him happy for only as long as the new car smell lasted. He belonged to a hunting club. He bought a speedboat and countless other trinkets, trying to make himself happy.

"But," said Tom, "I was miserable. I was smiling on

the outside but crying on the inside." And then, when he was forty-five years old, his devout sister pestered him into attending a Methodist laymen's conference at Lake Junaluska, North Carolina. Tom said that he went just to get her off his back. Tom figured he could survive that weekend of piety if he went properly prepared. So he packed his golf clubs and a large bottle of vodka into his white Cadillac, and off to Junaluska he went. There he met some laymen who had something he lacked. They obviously had real joy in their hearts and peace in their souls. Tom decided he wanted what they had.

One night he took a walk with one of those laymen. After a lengthy discussion, that layman said, in a loving way, "Tom, I'm afraid that if you died tonight, you would bust hell wide open." Tom knew he was right. He went back to his room, fell on his knees, and confessed his sin. Then he said, "Lord, I give as much of myself as I can to as much of you as I can understand."

At that moment, God worked the miracle of new birth in Tom Shipmon. God gave him a new attitude, new values, and a new sense of identity as a child of God. The blessed by-product of that new birth was an abiding joy and peace.

I first met Tom Shipmon when I moved to Memphis in the summer of 1994. At that point, Tom was in a hospital at the point of death, sometimes in a coma. We began to make his funeral plans. But even then, during his lucid moments, Tom was unintimidated by death and confident of heaven. The joy of the Lord filled his heart. Thanks be to God, Tom made a full recovery.

Tom is not perfect. His wife, Betty, would vouch for that. Like many of us, he is a forgiven sinner under reconstruction. But the most important fact about Tom Shipmon is that he has been born again.

It is God's desire that every person be born again. Only God can work that miracle. But all of us can place ourselves in a favorable position for God to reach us. How? By repenting of sin and trusting that Jesus Christ was God's Son who died on a cross for our sins. If we position ourselves accordingly, our Lord will not disappoint us. Jesus promised that "whoever comes to me I will never drive away" (John 6:37).

In *Just As I Am*, Billy Graham recalls meeting the theologian Karl Barth in Switzerland. When Graham preached in Basel, Barth attended the service. Graham's text for that service were the words of Jesus from the third chapter of John: "You must be born again." "I agreed largely with your sermon," Barth said afterward, "but I did not like that word *must*. I wish you could change that." Barth preferred that Graham simply declare that God had already acted. Graham decided to follow scripture. Later, Graham was in Zurich with Emil Brunner, also a theologian, who disagreed with Barth on the necessity of being born again. "Pay no attention to him," Brunner said. "Always put that word *must* in. A man *must* be born again."[6]

NOTES

1. John Wesley, *The Works of John Wesley Vol. 18: Journals and Diaries I (1735–38)*, ed. by W. Reginald Ward and Richard P. Heitzenrater (Nashville: Abingdon Press, 1988), p. 211.

2. Ibid., pp. 249-50.

3. John Wesley, *The Works of John Wesley Vol. 2: Sermons II (34-70)*, ed. by Albert C. Outler (Nashville: Abingdon Press, 1985), pp. 193-94.

4. John Wesley, *The Letters of the Rev. John Wesley, A.M. Vol. IV.* ed. by John Telford, B.A. (London: The Epworth Press, 1931), p. 332.

5. Wesley, *Works of John Wesley Vol. 2: Sermons II*, pp. 200-01.

6. Billy Graham, *Just As I Am: The Autobiography of Billy Graham* (HarperCollins, 1997), p. 694.

CHAPTER FIVE

RESTORING BELLS
TO OUR STEEPLES

Psalm 11:3-4, Jude 1-4, 17-21

When I was a youngster, I had a part-time job working for the church. It was convenient because I lived next door. Every Sunday I unlocked and locked the buildings and picked up trash in the sanctuary after worship. But the best part of my job was ringing the church bell early on Sunday mornings.

It must have been a huge bell up there in the belfry. The rope that rang it was about three times the size of a regular rope. It took considerable effort to get that bell to toll, but once I got it going, I could just jump up on the rope and ride it for a while. Not many churches have bells in their steeples anymore. Some churches have something more modern—a bell chime system that can be operated manually or by computer.

Let's think about bells of a different kind in church steeples. One of the characters in William Faulkner's novel *Light in August* asserts that "that which is destroying the Church is not the outward groping of those within it nor the inward groping of those without, but the professionals who control it and who have removed the bells from its steeples."[1] What a graphic way to describe the impotence of many mainline churches! They have lost or distorted the essential doctrines of the Christian faith. They are preaching and teaching the latest theological fads and New Age psychobabble. A prominent seminary president described what a dead mainline church looks like on Easter morning. The preacher stands in the pulpit and declares, "Christ is risen. Are you okay with that?" No bells are in their steeples ringing forth across city and countryside the only sure way to transform lives and save souls.

Stealing the bells from the church's steeples is not a new danger. Read the little Letter of Jude, written by our Lord's half–brother. Its basic purpose was to warn against false teachers who were trying to infiltrate the early church. Many of them did not believe that Jesus was God's Son. They also tried to lead the Christians into sinful practices. Jude called on the faithful Christians to "contend" for the faith. The Greek word for "contend" has military and wrestling connotations. It means to struggle or agonize for.

What are we supposed to contend for? "The faith that was once for all entrusted to the saints" (v. 3). Jude was referring to that body of doctrine passed down from Jesus through the apostles. The words "once for all" mean that the essentials of our faith are unchanging. Aren't you glad that we don't have to "reimagine" the faith every fifty years or so? To be loyal to that faith is orthodoxy. To depart from it is heresy.

Is heresy a real problem today? You be the judge. A prominent Los Angeles pastor was cited in a denominational magazine as challenging lay and clergy leaders to "change the theological code from Western-Christianity-only thinking (Jesus died to save us from our sins)" and to "forget our dogma of second coming and rapture," an "eschatology of the past" that does not serve us today.[2] I believe God is calling all mainline churches to restore the right theological bells to their steeples. Let me propose three bells that ought to ring in melodious and complementary harmony: the authority of scripture, the seriousness of sin, and the centrality of the cross.

The First Bell: The Authority of Scripture

In many seminaries today, the Bible is regarded as an interesting record of antiquity regarding the people of faith at rather primitive levels, but certainly not a dependable document for guiding the faith and ethics of modern people. Speaking at a United Methodist seminary, Marcus Borg, a fellow of the controversial Jesus Seminar, declared, "We need to be clear and candid. The Bible is a human product." If it is ascribed to divine inspiration, there will be "massive confusion."[3]

Any time you debate an issue of theology, in less than three minutes you come to the question of authority. What is it? Is it modern psychology, science, astrology, rationalism, or public opinion polls? I have found that if we ever move away from Holy Scripture as our authority, then we are left with nothing more than your opinion and mine, and neither one will buy you a cup of coffee.

The Bible says that every part of scripture is edifying; it declares that "the word of God is living and active" and that it is "sharper than any double-edged sword" (Hebrews 4:12).

In Billy Graham's awesome autobiography, *Just As I Am*, he described a pivotal moment in his ministry. It was in 1949, just before the Los Angeles crusade that would propel him to national fame. Graham was attending a retreat in the San Bernardino Mountains. Some apparent contradictions in scripture and some scholarly attacks on the Bible had troubled him. He awoke in the middle of the night, picked up his Bible, and walked outside. He placed that Bible on a tree stump and fell on his knees. Then he cried out, "Father, I am going to accept this as Thy Word—by *faith*! I'm going to allow faith to go beyond my intellectual questions and doubts, and I will believe this to be Your inspired Word."[4]

The Bible doesn't need our downsizing or apologizing or demythologizing; if we will just preach and teach it boldly, God can revive our dying mainline churches. If we must choose between unity and biblical truth, may God give us courage to side with truth.

The Second Bell: The Seriousness of Sin

Most mainline Protestants are uncomfortable with the truth about sin and the wrath of God. We prefer the warm and fuzzy world of grace. We prefer to say, "Now, now, it can't be all that bad. If you were baptized as a baby and try to be respectable and help us with this capital funds drive, God will surely grade on a curve and you'll slide into heaven, because God really is a sweetheart."

Universalism, the belief that there is no hell and everybody is going to heaven whether he or she wishes to or not, has cut the nerve of our evangelistic urgency. As early as 1990, Robert Morley, a United Methodist pastor on the West Coast, warned about the insidious cancer of universalism within his denomination. Writing in *The Christian Century*, he claimed that United Methodism had become committed to universalism. He wrote, "We no longer believe a decision for Christ matters much either in this life or the next. . . . We believe or hope that God is going to find a way to save everybody. . . . We don't talk about saving the lost or converting sinners . . . we speak of churching the unchurched."[5]

As Bishop Earl G. Hunt, Jr. points out, universalism goes back at least as far as the late–second century, but that it was "categorically repudiated" by John Wesley and by Bishops Coke and Asbury in the *1798 Disciplinary Notes*, "in which they called for resistance toward 'heretical doctrines,' noting especially Arianism, universalism, socialism, and other views contrary to Wesley's teaching."[6]

But some will say, "Wait a minute. God is love, and that love is incompatible with judgment and wrath." But then I think about the people who have loved me best across the years, especially my late father, himself a Methodist preacher. Papa's love for me was boundless, but he never felt that my lifestyle was off-limits for his judgment. And I have felt his wrath. But his wrath was an integral part of his love.

I recall a time as a teenager when I was driving much too fast. I was stopped by a lawman in Bishopville, South Carolina. In that little town, the policemen knew the young people by name. He lectured me for a while and then said, "Billy, I'm not going to fine you this time; but tomorrow I will stop by and say a word to Preacher Bouknight about this." I said, "Hold on, sir, if you don't mind, I would prefer to pay the fine. Whatever you do, don't talk to Papa."

You see, Papa hated with a white-hot intensity anything that could hurt me. That's the way God is. He is concentrated, pure righteousness and holiness. God hates sin with a seething passion, because he knows that it can wreck our lives and doom our eternal souls.

Today many mainline churches are not calling sinners to be redeemed; they are just rounding up respectable folks to help pay off the mortgage. Just imagine that you have had your annual physical examination and the doctor found a cancerous tumor. But let's suppose that he decided he would not tell you, because the news might upset you or distract you from your busy schedule. So he keeps his discovery a secret. He prescribes for you vitamin B tablets, exercise, and books on positive thinking. Once you discovered the truth, you would sue that doctor for malpractice. If, in the course of six months of preaching ministry, your pastor never declares that all of us are sinners who, apart from a personal relationship with Jesus Christ, are at risk of going straight to hell, you could sue him or her for malpractice.

The Third Bell: The Centrality of the Cross

The third and final bell to be replaced in our steeples is the centrality of the cross. Unless sin and hell are real threats, you don't need a cross. I have a pastor friend in Houston who says that if the cross were not absolutely necessary in order to save humanity, God would have been a monster to have allowed it. But there was and still is no other way by which we can be transformed and eternally saved.

How it must break God's loving heart to hear a seminary professor declare, "We don't need to hear about somebody hanging on a cross, and blood dripping, and all that stuff." Even worse, perhaps, when those words were spoken, the interdenominational audience exploded into applause.

The mystery of the cross! Who can begin to declare its full glory? Our puny minds cannot take it all in. Even Paul, with his massive intellect, confessed that he understood it only in part. But the central truth of the cross can be comprehended by a child. Peter expressed it as follows: "Christ died for sins once for all, the righteous for the unrighteous, to bring you to God" (1 Peter 3:18). The cross was so vital for Paul that he determined "to know nothing . . . except Jesus Christ and him crucified" (1 Corinthians 2:2). To the Galatians he declared, "May I never boast except in the cross of our Lord Jesus Christ" (Galatians 6:14).

I know this personally. I came into this world with a sin problem that I could not fix by myself. When Jesus died on that cross, he paid for my sin and made it possible for me to be reconciled to our holy and righteous God. The cross is my only hope of glory. The centrality of the cross must be a bell in our steeples.

Most so-called mainline churches are under tremendous pressure to compromise those essential biblical beliefs on which they were founded, and to embrace beliefs that are more politically correct and culturally comfortable. In an effort to resist that pressure, Christ United Methodist Church in Memphis affiliated with some fifteen hundred other United Methodist churches as part of the Confessing Movement. I am proud to be an officer in that unofficial United Methodist organization. Our shared purpose is to "contend for the faith that was once for all entrusted to the saints."

But having the right theological bells in our steeples is not enough. We do not have the power to set those bells ringing. Only God's mighty Holy Spirit can activate those bells. Only God can do the really big things: only God can save a lost person, only God can renew entire denominations, only God can reconcile the races in Memphis or any other city, and only God can bring peace to our public schools.

What can we do? We can pray fervently and faithfully. Then we can watch for God's initiatives and get with them. Remember the powerful promise of 2 Chronicles 7:14: "If my people, who are called by my name, will humble themselves and pray and seek my face and turn from their wicked ways, then will I hear from heaven and will forgive their sin and will heal their land."

Answer these questions honestly: Have you prayed for a single lost person by name this week? Have you prayed for your denomination and its leaders this week? Have you prayed for your local church and its pastor?

When the General Conference of The United Methodist Church met in 1956 in Minneapolis, race was the critical issue. Tension mounted. It seemed that the Methodist Church might split again, as had happened over one hundred years earlier, because of a racial issue. At that critical moment, the great evangelist Harry Denman stood and made a proposal. Harry proposed a twenty-four-hour prayer vigil at Wesley Methodist

Church, which was just a block away. People prayed there all through the night. One delegate said later that he would never forget the following day because the Holy Spirit rained down on the Conference and there was no more bitterness or bickering.

Only God can meet our deepest needs. If we pray fervently and faithfully, God will work wonders among us. Perhaps this is why Jude admonished the early church and us to "build yourselves up in your most holy faith and pray in the Holy Spirit" (v. 20). Ask God to hasten that day when the mainline churches of America can truly declare, "The bells are back in the steeples! And by the grace of God, they are ringing to high heaven!"

NOTES

1. William Faulkner, *Light in August* (New York: Vintage International, 1990), p. 487.

2. James E. Taylor, "Dismantling Racism," *Interpreter*, November/December 1994, pp. 10-11.

3. Quoted in Mark Tooley, "The Celebration of Unbelief," *Good News*, July/August 1999, p. 26.

4. Billy Graham, *Just As I Am: The Autobiography of Billy Graham* (San Francisco: HarperCollins, 1997), p. 139.

5. Robert Morley, "Confessions of a Naysayer," *The Christian Century*, February 7-14, 1990, p. 118.

6. Earl G. Hunt Jr., *Recovering the Sacred: Papers from the Sanctuary and the Academy* (Lake Junaluska: Jonathan Creek Press, 1992), p. 237. Bishop Hunt continues his discussion of universalism within The United Methodist Church on page 256.

CHAPTER SIX

THE SEDUCTIVENESS OF SODOM

Genesis 19:1-16

Do you remember the old fable of the frog that got cooked? According to the legend, someone wanted to cook a frog. But each time the frog was dropped into a pan of hot water, it jumped out. Then the cook got smart. She placed the frog in warm water. The frog relaxed. Then gradually, very gradually, the cook turned up the temperature of the stove. In fact, it happened so gradually that the frog never bothered to jump out. The frog got cooked.

That fable describes a tragic trend in American society. In 1931 the Supreme Court referred to America as a Christian nation. Yet in 1989, just fifty-eight years later, a federal judge noted in a decision that America is a secular nation. There was no howl of protest. What happened during those fifty-eight years? The secular humanists, vehemently opposed to Judeo-Christian values, had been turning up the temperature. Our spiritual values got cooked.

America's experience is not new or unique. Genesis 19 describes a similar process. The place was called Sodom, a prosperous city in the well-watered Jordan River Valley. Abraham's nephew, Lot, chose to live there even though "the men of Sodom were wicked and were sinning greatly against the LORD" (Genesis 13:13). We find out later that not even ten righteous men could be found in the large city of Sodom. A number of years pass. Lot becomes prominent in Sodom. He sits at the city gates with the other respected leaders. But Sodom has been influencing Lot more than Lot has been influencing Sodom.

One day two angels visited Sodom; they were disguised as men, and Lot did not recognize them. He thought they were just out-of-town travelers who needed hospitality. He invited them to spend the night at his home, but they declined, saying they would bed down in the public square. But Lot insisted that they go home with him, fearing the fate that would befall any man foolish enough to spend the night in Sodom's public square. The angels went to Lot's house for the night. But before bedtime, all the men of Sodom, both young and old, were pounding on Lot's door, demanding that the strangers be brought out so that they could be subjected to homosexual rape. The word "sodomy" comes from this biblical reference. It means unnatural sex or sex between two men.

Lot went out to try to reason with the lustful mob. He even offered his virgin daughters to the mob to use and abuse if they would just leave the strangers alone. Surely this shows how far Lot's ethical standards had fallen. But the mob was interested in sex with men, not sex with women. They tried to grab Lot, but the angels inside pulled him to safety. Then the angels blinded the men outside.

The angels told Lot that God was going to destroy the city because of its immorality. They urged Lot to gather his family and flee. But Lot's sons-in-law regarded the whole thing as a joke. Lot's wife and daughters were reluctant to leave; so was Lot. Sodom had grown on them. The angels had to literally grab them by the hands and pull them out of Sodom. Then came the destruction. The Lord rained down burning sulfur on Sodom. So complete was its destruction that even today archaeologists cannot pinpoint its exact location, though there is no doubt about its general locale.

Lot and his family were seduced by Sodom, but ever so gradually. The water temperature in the pan was raised very slowly. But for the grace of God, Lot would have been cooked like a frog. Let's ask if we today are like the proverbial frog, swimming around in the pan while the temperature is rising.

Think About Our Entertainment

In Memphis, where I live, we are becoming acclimated to the gambling industry in Tunica, Mississippi, just forty minutes south of us. Tunica is America's third most popular gambling resort. Tunica's public relations department is trying to train us to use the word "gaming" rather than "gambling." They first entice us to just come down for a show and a great meal. Then it's just a small step to the gambling tables.

Yes, we probably know that 10 percent of the people who dabble in gambling become addicted. Yes, we know that it violates the lesson we try to teach to our children—that you cannot get something for nothing. Yes, gambling plays a key role in Memphis's awful rate of bankruptcy, the highest in the nation. But you see, if television, radio, and the corporate world gradually hang a label of respectability on gambling, sooner or later we might agree that gambling really isn't so bad. The key is to turn up the temperature on the stove gradually.

There was a time when most movies were rated "PG" or "PG-13," with just a few rated "R." But have you looked lately? The vast majority of them are rated "R." Hollywood has made a calculated decision—that if you acclimate the public very gradually to profanity and sexual immorality, the public will not get alarmed. Hollywood producers believe that if they turn up the temperature very slowly, even Christians will pay to hear their God's holy name profaned.

The Value of a Human Life

Back in the 1960s, the abortionists started defending first-trimester abortions. Soon a Supreme Court decision legalized this practice. Before long, 1.6 million little unborn babies were being killed every year in America. Only a tiny fraction of these were instances of rape, incest, or danger to the mother. Most were situations in which the baby was deemed to be inconvenient.

Look how things have changed. Now there are abortionist leaders, including some church officials, who defend the right of a mother to take the life of an unborn child any time she wants. What has happened to us? The temperature on the stove has been turned up ever so gradually.

Sexual Behavior

This is the area in which Sodom earned its reputation. The biblical position is clear and unchanging: sex is reserved for the lifelong covenant of marriage between a man and a woman. Jesus endorsed such a view. He said, quoting from Genesis, "For this reason a man will leave his father and mother and be united to his wife, and the two will become one flesh" (Mark 10:7). The Bible's standard is fidelity within marriage and celibacy outside of marriage.

The Bible condemns adultery, homosexuality, and premarital sex (usually referred to in scripture as fornication). Our secular society disagrees. The message in movies and television is that sex is okay between any two people of either sex who are powerfully attracted to each other. In some schools teenagers are advised not to have sex, but are offered condoms as they leave class. That's like offering teens a class in safe driving and then handing them a radar detector as they complete the course.

Is the frog getting cooked? Yes! Today only 33 percent of American women and 25 percent of men say that sex is not okay before marriage. The rest have been convinced that premarital sex is fine, despite the fact that couples who live together before marriage are 33 percent more likely to divorce than those who do not. Sodom is seductive. The temperature of the water is rising.

One of the most disturbing parts of the President Clinton–Monica Lewinksy affair was the argument made by some that the act of committing adultery and lying about it is so common that it is not as bad as really serious sins. What a commentary on our society!

The media is trying to teach us that nice, respectable, intellectual people do not condemn homosexual behavior. If one does, one must be ignorant or homophobic. Therefore, when the Reverend Reggie White, formerly of the Green Bay Packers, declares the biblical view that homosexuality is a sin, he is castigated in the media. The homosexual lobby is having an impact. Seven percent of American companies now treat same-sex couples among their employees as though they were married, giving them marital benefits.

The end result of this rush toward Sodom is what we see in San Francisco. Recently, the city council voted to require all private businesses to offer domestic partners any employee benefits they extend to married couples. The water temperature is rising, and the soul of our society is the frog. Sodom is so very seductive.

There is an alternative to just sitting around and watching the frog get cooked. We can become proactive Christians, cheerfully aggressive and biblically grounded, unashamed and unembarrassed to stand for Christ and his values. We must be salt, light, and leaven in our pagan culture. We must be partisans in the occupied territory of secularism. Some things we can do are rather simple. When you have a business lunch, be bold enough to offer to say a blessing for the group. In daily conversation, give thanks to God. Do you remember how the great baseball player Mark McGwire slipped in a word of witness when he was chasing the home run record in 1998? After hitting home run number 61, he told the press that on the day he died, he hoped that, after seeing the Lord, he could talk to Roger Maris and Babe Ruth. The network managers don't like references to faith, but they just could not find a way to cut that out!

Do you keep a Bible on your work desk? If not, why not? Are you willing to sacrifice seeing this year's Academy Award–winning movie so as not to subsidize the profaning of God's holy name? When you hear someone profane God's holy name, especially if the two of you are alone, say to that person, "If you knew how much God loves you, you could not use his name that way."

If you're a teenager, would you be willing to join a movement like "True Love Waits," making a decision to save sex for marriage? Stand up for the Bible's sexual standard as God's recipe for marital happiness and sexual fulfillment.

Choose carefully how you spend your money. Support companies that support Christian values. Penalize those that do not. Recently, I wrote to the president of a large soup company. I said, "Sir, since you have decided that Reggie White is not good enough to advertise your soup, I have decided that your soup is not good enough for my family." We Christians have a duty to affirm the Bible's position that homosexuality is wrong. If your company wants to treat same-sex couples as though they were married, protest! Such a policy dignifies sin and demeans marriage.

But we must avoid a favorite strategy of the devil— that is, to drive us to the opposite extreme. There must be no room in a Christian's heart or conduct for animosity toward homosexual persons. They are precious creations of God, just like the rest of us. They are sinners, just like the rest of us. Homosexually oriented persons will find it far easier to live morally upright lives if they are loved and included in the church community. All of us sinners need other believers who love us unreservedly even while they hate our sin.

Sodom is always seductive. The water temperature on the stove is rising. We must not sit idly by and get cooked. Instead, let us go on the offensive. In the name of Christ, let's change this culture. God will help us fulfill what we pray for every Sunday: "Thy kingdom come on earth as it is in heaven."

Richard Halverson, former pastor of Fourth Presbyterian Church in Washington, D.C., was flying into his home city one evening about dusk. As the plane descended, he tried to locate the lights of his church building. He saw the lights of the Department of Labor, the White House, and the Capitol. But he was disappointed that he could not locate the lights of Fourth Presbyterian. Then a marvelous thought came to him. He remembered that the church is not a particular building, but that the church is wherever its people are. They were spread all over the city, some at the Justice Department, some at Commerce, some at the State Department. Wherever they were, the lights of the church were on.[1]

And so may it be with Christians in my city, in your city, in this nation, and around the world!

NOTE

1. Charles Colson, *The Body* (Dallas: Word Publishing, 1992), pp. 271-72.

CHAPTER SEVEN

MARY'S REVOLUTIONARY SONG

Luke 1:46-55

At home I have a yellowing copy of one of the world's most revolutionary documents. In it are found these immortal words: "We hold these truths to be self-evident, that all men are created equal." That document, the Declaration of Independence, is the charter of the American Revolution. Though we have not yet lived up to it, it is still the vision that inspires us.

The only document I know that is more revolutionary is in our Bible. It is called the Magnificat, and is found in Luke 1, verses 46 through 55. Before India won its independence, it was under British rule. Bishop William Temple of the Anglican Church warned his missionaries to India not to read the Magnificat in public. He feared that it would be so inflammatory that it might start a revolution!

The document is all the more remarkable when one remembers that it came from the lips of a simple teenaged girl named Mary. She grew up in the obscure village of Nazareth in what is now northern Israel. The angel Gabriel appeared to Mary and announced that she had been chosen to be the mother of the long-awaited Messiah. Gabriel told Mary that her Aunt Elizabeth, well past childbearing age, had become pregnant. Immediately Mary went to visit Elizabeth. Under the influence of the Holy Spirit, both women sensed that God had chosen them for special tasks and would do great things through their children.

The Holy Spirit then gave Mary insights far too profound for a simple teenager to originate. She declared the impact that her son would have upon the world. She announced three distinct revolutions that Jesus would instigate and activate.[1] She spoke of these revolutions in the past tense, as if they had already happened. The world has been reeling ever since under the influence of our revolutionary Lord.

The First Revolution of Jesus Is Spiritual in Nature

In verse 51 we read that "he has scattered those who are proud in their inmost thoughts." Many American mainline Protestants have a pride problem. I once heard the late Bishop Robert Goodrich say that some of his church members in Dallas were so self-righteous that they had to hold onto the pews to keep from ascending. Our problem is not that we are unaware of our sin. We know our frailties. But deep down we believe we are so much better than most folks that God would be ashamed of himself not to let us into heaven on good behavior. When push comes to shove, we believe that God will grade on the curve. But the Bible says that the wages of sin is death (Romans 6:23). Quoting from Psalm 14, Paul says that "there is no one who does good, not even one" (Romans 3:12). Not even Mother Teresa made it to heaven on merit. That truth ought to banish our pride and humble us a bit.

Bill Hybels, pastor of the great Willow Creek Church, was on a plane one day. The man seated beside him struck up a conversation. Upon finding out that Bill was a clergyman, the man said, "Well, I believe in God but I don't affiliate with any church. Don't really think I need it. Sure, I make some mistakes but I live respectably and give to charities. I wouldn't hurt a soul on purpose. I believe that God will accept me on that basis."

Bill took out a legal pad and said, "Let's make a grading scale for all people, from one to ten, with ten being just about perfect. Who are the best people in the world?" The man thought for a moment and said, "Mother Teresa and Billy Graham." "Okay," said Bill. "But we must allow them to place themselves on our chart. Each of them has said, 'I am a sinner and have no chance of salvation unless it is a gift to me from Christ.' So, by their own admission, they deserve to be down near the bottom of the chart. Now, my next question is, where should we put you on the chart? You don't want to be above Mother Teresa, do you?" The man replied, "If Mother Teresa is not good enough to get into heaven, I guess I'm in worse shape than I thought." Then Bill Hybels drew a cross right across the middle of the chart. Underneath that cross he wrote these words from 1 John 2:1-2: "But if anybody does sin, we have one who speaks to the Father in our defense—Jesus Christ, the Righteous One. He is the atoning sacrifice for our sins." Beneath the verse he drew a line and said to the man beside him, "Just sign here if you would like to be covered by the sacrifice of Christ on the cross. Then you can be as sure of going to heaven as Mother Teresa." The man signed on the dotted line.

The first revolution of Jesus is to banish pride and spiritual self-sufficiency. None of us has any hope until we dump our trash at the foot of the cross.

The Second Revolution of Jesus Is Social in Nature

In verse 52 we read, "He has brought down rulers from their thrones but has lifted up the humble." God seems always to be overturning the world's social order. He helped a band of Hebrew slaves defeat an Egyptian pharaoh. He took a humble shepherd boy and made him Israel's greatest king. And when he sought a woman to be the mother of the Messiah, he chose a lower-class teenager from a hick town.

Rank and caste and class are always under attack when Jesus is around. Hear the words of Paul to the Galatians: "All of you who were baptized into Christ have clothed yourselves with Christ. There is neither Jew nor Greek, slave nor free, male nor female, for you are all one in Christ Jesus" (Galatians 3:27-28).

In 1955, Rosa Parks ignited a revolution when she refused to yield her bus seat to a white male. God was on her side. God opposes every ruling system that devalues people or deprives them of life, liberty, or justice.

How dare we value God's people differently based on skin pigmentation? When we treat someone as being of lesser value because of race, that is sin; whether it takes the form of a realtor not wanting to sell a certain house to an African American, someone telling a racist joke at a cocktail party, an African American politician calling whites "devils," or comments that devalue Jews, all of it is sin.

Today there are two contrary movements in the city where I live. One is a desire to isolate oneself from all that is negative in the city. The negative is usually associated with the poor and the black. The isolationists want to keep their schools, neighborhoods, and government as undefiled by the poor and black as possible. The attitude is that the "negative elements" of the city can take care of themselves, just keep us as far away as possible.

But there is another movement, and I believe it is inspired by Jesus Christ. It is a reconciliation movement. It declares that every person is created in God's image and for him or her Jesus died. Therefore, we must not write off that three-year-old growing up in the run-down apartment or that drug addict who spent last night on a bench in a public park. We dare not isolate ourselves from the poor because that is where Jesus is. The Bible tilts in the direction of the widow and the orphan, "the least of these brothers of mine" (Matthew 25:40).

The Third Revolution of Jesus Is Economic in Nature

In verse 53 we read, "He has filled the hungry with good things but has sent the rich away empty." The Bible is tough on us who, in relation to the rest of the world, are rich. Jesus said that "it is easier for a camel to go through the eye of a needle than for a rich man to enter the kingdom of God" (Matthew 19:24).

A Christian society is one in which no person dares to have too much while others have too little. Methodist founder John Wesley both preached and practiced this principle, as illustrated by the way he spent Christmas in his eighty-second year:

> At this season we usually distribute coals and bread among the poor of society [in London]. But I now considered, they wanted clothes, as well as food. So on this, and the four following days, I walked through the town, and begged two hundred pounds, in order to clothe them that needed it most. But it was hard work, as most of the streets were filled with melting snow, which often lay ankle deep; so that my feet were steeped in snow-water nearly from morning till evening.[2]

If we die with a lot of money in investments, leaving huge amounts to children who don't really need it, while people in our communities are homeless, hungry, and in despair, God will surely call us to account. Let's suppose that you have three grown children. One son is a company vice president in Atlanta, earning $200,000 a year. Your daughter is doing quite well as a surgeon in Miami. Your other son is an alcoholic in Richmond, living hand-to-mouth, unable to hold a steady job. As a parent, where would your focus be? On Richmond, of course. And I'm certain you would call those prosperous children in Miami and Atlanta to help their less fortunate brother.

God is a good heavenly father. His focus is always on his children with the biggest problems and fewest resources. And he calls us, his other children, to lend a hand. This should be the big question for each of us: How can I help the poor in such a way that I build up their confidence and promote their independence? We don't need more government welfare schemes. We need Christian entrepreneurs with imagination who are utterly committed to Christ and the poor.

Does your company have high school youth from disadvantaged backgrounds working for you during the summers, learning the basics of success? Are you investing in college and technical scholarships for deserving disadvantaged persons? Does your company hire and promote women and minorities just because it's right? Over the last twenty years, thousands of poor people have been given small loans at low interest rates so that they can start new businesses. These loans, provided by Christian corporate leaders, ranged from $75 to $500, the kind of loan they could not get from a bank, but only perhaps from a high interest loan shark. The results of these investments have transformed some communities. Wouldn't it be wonderful if every company had such a loan fund for innovative investments among the poor?

Every affluent church needs poor people in its membership. We need them more than they need us. Why? So that Jesus will feel at home among us. After all, when God became flesh, he chose to be one of the *am ha'aretz*—the people of the land, the poor folks.

What the church where I serve is doing in a low income area of our city is not just for the folks who live in that area. It is for us too. If we do not identify with the poor, Jesus will not identify with us. And if we try to be a church without Jesus, we will be nothing more than a religious feel-good club for the pious and the proud.

Historians still consider the successful American Revolution something of a miracle. George Washington and his little ragtag army had to fight the mighty British and their hired troops from Germany. Not only that, they were opposed by many Americans. In many states there were more Tories (pro–British Americans) than rebels.

The Jesus Revolution faces a similar problem. Some of Jesus' toughest opposition is within the church. Many church members claim to be followers of Jesus, but say in their hearts, "Don't make any big changes. I'm doing pretty well with the present system. Don't rock the boat."

What about you? In regard to the Jesus Revolution, are you a rebel or a Tory? Which do you love more—this world or the kingdom of God? Is your heart with Jesus or with your stocks and bonds?

NOTES

1. William Barclay, *The Gospel of Luke* (Philadelphia: The Westminster Press, 1956), pp. 9-10.

2. John Wesley, *The Works of the Rev. John Wesley, A.M. Vol. IV* (London: Wesleyan Conference Office, 1872), p. 295.

CHAPTER EIGHT

THE WORD OF GOD: TRUTH DIVINE

Hebrews 4:12-13

The following advertisement was posted in the window of a Christian bookstore:

> "The Word of God—truth divine.
> Leather bound, only $7.99.
> It scares the devil when he sees
> Bibles sold as cheap as these."

The author of the biblical Letter to the Hebrews described the word of God as sharper than the sharpest instrument of his time—the double–edged sword. The divinely inspired scriptures of the Bible have the awesome power to cut through all our rubbish and disguises and pretensions. The words of the Bible, carried on the wings of the Holy Spirit, can plumb the depths of our minds, healing and convicting and comforting.

The Letter to the Hebrews was addressed to the Christians of Jewish background who lived in Rome. It may be the earliest sermon in the entire New Testament.

Most American mainline Protestants believe that the entire Bible was inspired by God. Paul assured Timothy (and us) that every word in the Bible is there to serve some good purpose in our growth as Christians (2 Timothy 3:16). The newest book in the Bible is at least nineteen centuries old. Nevertheless, the Bible remains the all-time bestseller. It is the most quoted book in the world. More than eleven hundred languages and dialects now claim the Bible as their own.

Most mainline Protestants do not read the Bible with a crude kind of literalism. When the Bible tells us that the faithful will be able to handle dangerous snakes (Mark 16:18), we do not interpret that to mean that we should grab rattlesnakes.

When the Bible is read intelligently and under the guidance of the Holy Spirit, it is our final authority for faith and ethics. I believe that it is free from significant error. If God inspired the writing of the Bible, it can be assumed that he would protect it from falsehood.

One of the devil's greatest victories is his ability to persuade many people, inside and outside the church, that the Bible is less than authoritative. Some seminary professors teach that much of it is just myth. Some preachers, unsure of biblical authority, have no life-changing, soul-saving gospel to proclaim.

Dr. Marcus J. Borg, professor at Oregon State University, member of the Jesus Seminar, and frequent speaker at mainline Protestant seminaries, sees the Bible and the person of Jesus as a "helpful 'lens' through which to view the sacred." Further, he states that modern people rightly are "suspicious that any particular collection of teachings or doctrines can be absolute truth." According to Borg, every notion of truth is "conditioned and relative to the time and place in which it originated."[1] As already noted (in chapter 5), Borg also believes that attributing divine inspiration to the Bible will lead to confusion.

But Borg is contradicted by Paul, who asserted that all scripture is inspired by God, or "God-breathed" (2 Timothy 3:16).

I like the story of a Christian businesswoman who was

reading her Bible one day on an airplane. She happened to be sitting beside a skeptic. When he noticed her Bible, he chuckled and said to her, "You look much too bright to believe the stuff that is in that book." With a smile she replied, "Of course I believe this book; it's the Bible."

He replied, "Well, what about that guy who was swallowed by a whale?" She said, "His name was Jonah. Yes, I believe it."

"Tell me this," said the man. "How did Jonah survive all that time inside the whale?" She replied, "Well, I don't know. But when I get to heaven, I'll ask him."

With some sarcasm the man said, "But what if he isn't in heaven?" With a warm smile, she replied, "Then you can ask him."

Bishop William Ragsdale Cannon, one of America's most brilliant church leaders and seminary deans of the twentieth century, was supportive of Wesley's high view of scripture and warned against changing the holy book:

> The Bible then is God's gift to us, not a book humans have composed for themselves and given to themselves for their own edification. It is God's chart for their happiness and satisfaction here, and their blessedness in heaven. Therefore to change one jot or one tittle of it, to try to make it conform to some human interest, concern, or cause is to risk damnation. We are to receive it as it is written, with open hearts and eager minds, and through it to be instructed in the ways of God. To attempt to rewrite it or in any way modify it from a racist, feminist, liberationist, liberal, conservative, or any other perspective not its own is the most dangerous of all heresies.[2]

If revival is going to come to an individual, church, or nation, it will be fueled by a rediscovery of God's Holy Word. I pray that the Holy Spirit will lead us into a deeper appreciation of and attention to the inspired book called the Bible.

The Word of God Is Living and Active

Turn with me now to Hebrews 4, verse 12. The Bible is no dead manuscript from ancient history. It is more relevant than the morning newspaper. You can't truly understand *USA Today* unless you read it from a biblical perspective.

It would be hard to get many people to study the words of, for example, Herodotus, the ancient Greek historian. But literally millions of Bible study groups meet each week around the world. Why? Because the Bible is not a history book; rather, it is God's pipeline into the here and now.

Countless individuals have found themselves alone in a motel room. For some reason, they took that Gideon Bible from the drawer beside the bed, opened it, and began reading. Suddenly their lives were changed! Why? Because the book in their hands was God-breathed.

The famous French skeptic Voltaire once said that within a hundred years the Bible would be a forgotten book found only in museums. By the time that one hundred years had passed, Voltaire's home, in which he had made this statement, had been occupied by the Geneva Bible Society. God must have smiled! As Jesus said, "Heaven and earth will pass away, but my words will never pass away" (Matthew 24:35).

Holy Scripture Is Piercing and Penetrating

"Sharper than any double-edged sword, it penetrates even to dividing soul and spirit. . . . Nothing in all creation is hidden from God's sight" (Hebrews 4:12-13). Like a surgeon's scalpel, the Word of God gets into the little tight places, the hidden recesses of our hearts and minds.

I have been at hundreds of funerals. I have looked into the eyes of people so devastated by grief that they could hardly speak. Not all the good advice of Billy Graham, Robert Schuller, and the Pope put together could drive away their hurt. But it is amazing how the following words, three thousand years old, can reach to the aching depths of their pain and bring relief: "The LORD is my shepherd; I shall not be in want. . . . Even though I walk through the valley of the shadow of death, I will fear no evil, for you are with me." Oh, how that Twenty-third Psalm can penetrate!

The Bible can also pierce and penetrate in order to convict and to cleanse us. As surely as a good dentist finds a particular tooth that has a problem, Holy Scripture reaches and reveals those parts of us that need God's healing.

Many people who, like us, appear to be respectable, have sordid secrets hidden away that they hope will never see the light of day. Many men keep pornographic magazines stashed in a desk drawer or some other hideaway. Some use the Internet as a way to wallow in filth. Some of us have greed or racism stashed away in hidden places of the heart.

The Bible penetrates those secret places with words like these from Paul: "Whatever is true, whatever is noble, whatever is right, whatever is pure, whatever is lovely, whatever is admirable—if anything is excellent or praiseworthy—think about such things" (Philippians 4:8).

The Bible reaches every nook and cranny of our lives, demanding full disclosure to God and, often, accountability to other people.

The Bible Judges the Thoughts and Attitudes of the Heart

During the Ivana and Donald Trump divorce, Marla Maples was asked about her religious roots. She said that she believed in the Bible, but added that "you can't always take [it] literally and be happy."[3] Marla was right in one respect—the God of the Bible will not let a person be happy without being holy.

If I am unwilling to forgive someone who asks for forgiveness, the Bible makes me feel like that elder brother in the story of the prodigal son, hard-hearted and vengeful.

If I give my country club more money each year than I give to the church, then I am judged by that widow of scripture who gave her last penny to God.

When I begin to mentally prepare a list of those who are surely going to hell, the words of Jesus haunt me: "Do not judge, or you too will be judged" (Matthew 7:1).

When I hold a grudge against my business competitor or an in-law or someone who mistreated my child, the words of Jesus indict me: "But if you do not forgive men their sins, your Father will not forgive your sins" (Matthew 6:15).

President Bill Clinton was impeached because of a moral failure that he thought would never be known. When that failure was discovered, his reaction was tragically wrong. The President will finally be judged, not by the Congress or the American people, but by God. And God will use a document far greater than the Constitution. God will use the timeless standards of Holy Scripture.

The same Bible that judges President Clinton also judges our attitude toward him. It's easy for us to feel a bit smug and think, *That couldn't happen to me.* But Jesus asked, "Why do you look at the speck of sawdust in your brother's eye and pay no attention to the plank in your own eye?" (Matthew 7:3). We sinners must be careful in denouncing other sinners.

Someone once made a profound statement that I think I will always remember. He said that we are capable of doing anything anyone else has ever done, given the right circumstances and without the grace of God.

Because the Bible is our guidebook and yardstick, shouldn't we immerse ourselves in it?

Let me challenge us to invest at least twenty minutes a day in a four-step recovery of Holy Scripture.

- First, as you prepare to open the Bible, pray a few moments for God's inspiration and for understanding.
- Second, read at least five verses. Start with the New Testament, and use a modern translation, like the New International Version.
- Third, after you read, ask if there is a truth in what you have read that God wants you to receive and live by.
- Fourth, thank God for that truth and proceed into a time of prayer.

Those twenty minutes a day can revolutionize your life.

That great Australian Christian, Alan Walker, used to tell a story about Pitcairn Island in the Pacific. About two hundred years ago, some of the men responsible for the mutiny on the *Bounty* came to Pitcairn along with some Tahitian natives. They settled on the island, but almost destroyed themselves under the influence of sex and alcohol. Eventually, there were a number of murders, a suicide, and an accidental death, until John Adams was left as the last survivor of the *Bounty*.

One day, as Adams rummaged through a chest from the ship, he found a Bible. As he read it, says Walker, "a miracle happened: the new life of God came into his heart." John Adams began to teach the others the Christian faith, an act that transformed the island.[4] Today it is a healthy, vibrant, Christian community. It all started with the discovery of a Bible.

The author of Hebrews challenges us as individuals and as a nation to rediscover the book of all books. I invite you to share with me John Wesley's affirmation: "O give me that book! At any price give me the Book of God! I have it. Here is knowledge enough for me. Let me be *homo unius libri* [a man of one book]."[5]

NOTES

1. Mark Tooley, "The Celebration of Unbelief," *Good News*, July/August 1999, p. 27.

2. William Ragsdale Cannon, *A Magnificent Obsession* (Nashville: Abingdon Press, 1999), pp. 361-62.

3. Quoted in Charles Colson, *The Body* (Dallas: Word Publishing, 1992), p. 118.

4. Alan Walker, *Jesus the Liberator* (Nashville: Abingdon Press, 1973), pp. 11-12.

5. John Wesley, *The Works of John Wesley Vol. I: Sermons I (1-33)*, ed. by Albert C. Outler (Nashville: Abingdon Press, 1984), p. 105.

CHAPTER NINE

JESUS REPLACED SOMEONE
AT CALVARY

Mark 15:6-15

One day a man called a church by mistake. The church receptionist happened to be distracted at the time, and did not answer the phone in the usual fashion. She just said "Hello." The man said, "I want to order one pound of barbecue, two pints of cole slaw, and a dozen hush puppies." The receptionist said, "Wait a minute, sir. We are not a food service operation. You must have the wrong number." The man hesitated a moment and then asked, "What do you sell? What business are you in?"

That's a fair question. What is the church selling? What is the principal message we declare or the primary goal we seek? Is the church's primary purpose to improve the morality of the community in which it is located? Are we here just to offer spiritual first aid to our members when they go through hard times? Is our main message that if you keep the Ten Commandments, life will be better?

No! Here is our bottom line. We are giving away—not selling—this truth: Jesus Christ came down from heaven to save us from our sins by his sacrificial death on the cross. That is the central message of the whole Bible.

There is a name for that truth: the doctrine of the Atonement. If you look up "atonement" in the dictionary, it will tell you that the word means a satisfaction or reparation for a wrong or injury. For example, in the midst of war hysteria in 1942, we relocated about 100,000 Japanese Americans to internment centers on the West Coast. We realized later that such action violated our own Bill of Rights. In recent years we have paid money to Japanese Americans who were held in internment centers. Such payment is an atonement for the wrong we did them.

Atonement in a spiritual context refers to the reconciliation of God and humanity by means of the life, suffering, and death of Jesus Christ. John Wesley, founder of Methodism, referred to this as the central doctrine of the Christian faith. The truth of the Atonement is expressed this way in 1 John 4:10: "God . . . loved us and sent his Son as an atoning sacrifice for our sins." Bishop William R. Cannon described Atonement as follows:

> God loves us even while we are sinners and desires to forgive us and make us his sons and daughters in the household of faith. He is a merciful God, but at the same time he is a God of justice, and his justice must be fully satisfied before he can exercise his mercy. He forgives us our sins, but only for the sake of Jesus Christ who became sin for us and requites God's wrath by accepting the punishment of our sins. The fact that God would impose guilt on him and punish him through crucifixion for our sin seems unjust and wicked and unworthy of the character of God. And so it would be if Jesus were not himself God, so that in his crucifixion it is God who suffers and dies on our behalf.[1]

We sing the great truth of the Atonement with the words of that wonderful old hymn by Robert Lowry:

> What can wash away my sin?
> Nothing but the blood of Jesus.
> What can make me whole again?
> Nothing but the blood of Jesus.

On the day that Jesus was executed, there was one man in Jerusalem who learned the truth of the

Atonement before anybody else. His name was Barabbas. His story is told in Mark 15. Let's go back to Jerusalem at the time of Jesus' death. Remember, this was an occupied province of the mighty Roman Empire. The Jews of Palestine hated their Roman occupiers and were constantly plotting espionage and subversion. In an effort to placate the Jews, the Romans had a custom of releasing one prisoner each year during the Jewish festival of Passover. Verse 6 of Mark 15 refers to that custom. The Roman governor Pontius Pilate selected one prisoner to be set free.

Verse 7 tells us that one of the prisoners being held by the Romans was a fanatical nationalist named Barabbas. A violent man, he had pledged to murder every Roman he could. He had been convicted of robbery and murder. In verse 8 we are introduced to the crowd that had gathered outside Pilate's office. This was a very different group from the one that had welcomed Jesus to Jerusalem just a few days earlier. That earlier Sunday assembly was composed of pious pilgrims, but this mob outside Pilate's office had come to lobby for Barabbas. They loved the bravery and patriotism of this man who dared to kill the hated Romans. Also mixed into this crowd were followers and servants of the high priests who wanted to get rid of Jesus. Suddenly the interests of the two groups converged in a way that spelled trouble for Jesus.

In verse 9, Pilate asks the crowd, "Do you want me to release to you the king of the Jews?" He mentions Jesus, not by name, but by his popular title, "king of the Jews." Perhaps Pilate thought that Jesus' popularity with the masses would win his release over a fanatical murderer. But Pilate had misjudged this crowd. They shouted, "Give us Barabbas." And then, when asked what should be done with Jesus, they screamed, "Crucify him, crucify him!"

On that morning, Barabbas was a dead man walking. He was facing the horror of crucifixion, a method of execution so painful that a new word was invented to describe it—"excruciating." But at the last possible moment, Jesus took his place.

Barabbas was not unique. You and I were as good as dead in our sins, without any way of curing our spiritual sickness. Left to our own devices, we were headed for a life of inner discord and dysfunctional relationships, and an eternity in hell. But then, Jesus took our place. What he did on Calvary's cross is as potent today as it was in the first century.

The doctrine of the Atonement is under attack today. But that is nothing new. Paul noted that even in the first century, the preaching of the cross was regarded as foolishness to many (1 Corinthians 1:18). In the eighteenth century, John Wesley declared that "as long as the world stands, there will be a thousand objections to this scriptural doctrine. For still the preaching of *Christ crucified* will be foolishness to the wise men of the world."[2] In a letter to William Law, Wesley was extremely critical because he "failed to find in Law's writings the gospel pronouncement of Christ's atoning work for man." For Wesley, faith in the Atonement was the only way to be saved.[3]

Today numerous theologians and seminary professors reject the Atonement. One referred to it recently as "divine child abuse." As noted earlier, another declared, "We don't need to hear about somebody hanging on a cross, and blood dripping, and all that stuff." And when she made that statement, the interdenominational audience exploded into applause.

Thanks be to God, our beliefs are not dictated by some radical, truth-denying professors. Our beliefs are anchored in God's Holy Word. Note what the Bible says about the cross and the Atonement:

- John the Baptist said with reference to Jesus: "Look, the Lamb of God, who takes away the sin of the world!" (John 1:29).
- "[Jesus] is the atoning sacrifice for our sins, and not only for ours but also for the sins of the whole world" (1 John 2:2).
- Paul wrote to the Corinthians, saying, "God made him who had no sin to be sin for us, so that in him we might become the righteousness of God" (2 Corinthians 5:21).

Let me try to put the Atonement in my own words. God loves us immensely, but hates our sin with a passion. God hates our sin as a parent hates the malignant tumor that threatens his or her child's life. Because God is just and holy and altogether righteous, he cannot ignore sin. Sin is a direct challenge to everything God represents.

In this world that God built on righteous foundations, sin cannot be forgiven and set aside unless somebody pays for it. Only God was great enough and good enough to make atonement for the sins of the whole world. So God came to earth as a man named Jesus. He became the scapegoat for the sins of the world. He took Barabbas's place on the cross. He took my place on the cross. He took your place on the cross. "For God so loved the world that he gave his one and only Son, that whoever believes in him shall not perish but have eternal life" (John 3:16).

Harry Blamires uses a helpful metaphor for the Atonement. He suggests that we think of the human race as the passengers aboard a hijacked jetliner flying through time. God himself directed its takeoff from the divine control tower. Somehow the devil managed to get a boarding pass. When the plane reached cruising altitude, the devil produced his weapons, threatened the pilot, and took control of the aircraft. Thus the plane flew on fearfully through history from airport to airport until it was caught on the tarmac at Jerusalem, an outpost of the Roman Empire, in the reign of Tiberius Caesar. There the Son of God offered himself as sole hostage in exchange for the passengers and crew. That is the truth of the Atonement.

The heart of the Christian faith is the declaration that the Son of God died in our place. How can you be sure that you are a Christian, that you have been saved, and that you are on the way to heaven? Do you admit that you have a sin problem that you cannot fix by yourself? Do you believe that Jesus died in your place on Calvary's cross? In gratitude, have you invited Jesus to be the leader of your life?

If your answer to these questions is yes, you have been forgiven and saved. There is a great Charles Wesley hymn that declares this central truth of our faith:

> O Love divine, what hast thou done!
> The immortal God hath died for me!
> The Father's co-eternal Son
> bore all my sins upon the tree.
> Th'immortal God for me hath died:
> My Lord, my Love, is crucified!
>
> Is crucified for me and you,
> to bring us rebels back to God.
> Believe, believe the record true,
> ye all are bought with Jesus' blood.
> Pardon for all flows from his side:
> My Lord, my Love, is crucified!

NOTES

1. William Ragsdale Cannon, *A Magnificent Obsession* (Nashville: Abingdon Press, 1999), p. 364.

2. Quoted by Steve Harper, "Cross Purposes: Wesley's View of the Atonement," *Basic United Methodist Beliefs: An Evangelical View* (Wilmore, Ky.: Good News Books, 1986), p. 39.

3. Robert W. Burtner and Robert E. Chiles, eds., *John Wesley's Theology: A Collection from His Works* (Nashville: Abingdon, 1982), p. 73.

CHAPTER TEN

JESUS AND JUDGMENT

Romans 2:11-16

When I was a youngster of seven or eight years of age, our neighborhood grocery store was owned by a Mr. Strout. He knew our family well. One day when I was in the store, I saw a customer walk up to the counter with an armful of groceries and say, "Charge it, Mr. Strout." No money was exchanged. He just said "charge it" and walked out. I was amazed by this mysterious transaction. I said to myself, "How foolish I have been, believing that money was required for needed items, when all I had to do was say the magic words *charge it.*"

So I began using those magic words regularly, and they worked. I began bringing my friends to the store, inviting them to get whatever they wanted. I felt like a politician in Washington. I had a license to spend.

But one day I heard my father call out the name "William," which was always an ominous sign. He ushered me into the dining room and there, spread out on the table, were all those charge slips, one for every single time I had said "Charge it." Papa accepted my story that I had acted out of ignorance. Otherwise, the punishment would have been worse. As it was, I had to work off every one of those charge slips by doing chores. And I had to make a personal apology to Mr. Strout. That was one of my earliest encounters with judgment. I learned that the charge slips always come home. Some other types of correspondence may get lost in the U.S. Mail, but the charge slips always get through.

The Bible teaches that judgment is part of God's created order. Because God is righteous, judgment is the divine reaction to sin. In Romans 1:18, Paul declared: "The wrath [or judgment] of God is being revealed from heaven against all the godlessness and wickedness of men." In most mainline Protestant churches it is not politically correct to talk about judgment. We subcontract that job to the Southern Baptists. Most mainline churches prefer the warm and fuzzy message of grace. But any message of grace that skips judgment is sloppy *agape*, or cheap grace.

The highest virtue for most mainline Protestants is tolerance. But tolerating anything that God's Word says is intolerable is like keeping rattlesnakes in our homes as pets. Their coloring may be pretty, but they are deadly.

When we deal with Jesus and judgment, we are in one of those good news and bad news situations. The bad news of the gospel is that judgment is coming as surely as night follows day. The good news is that there is a way to bypass judgment; it was provided by the cross.

The scriptural focus for our thoughts on Jesus and judgment is the second chapter of Paul's Letter to the Romans, beginning with verse 11. Let me set the scene for you. The year is approximately A.D. 58. Paul is in the city of Corinth, on the southern tip of Greece. He is writing a letter to the Christians in the city of Rome. He does not know these people personally; he has never visited Rome. However, he hopes to visit them soon and perhaps use Rome as a base for evangelizing regions to the west, like Spain. Therefore, he writes to the Romans in order to introduce himself and his gospel. In chapter 2, Paul declares three vital truths about Jesus and judgment.

Judgment Is Guaranteed

Judgment is as certain as the sunrise. Some of it is immediate; some is delayed; and the rest will come at the end of this life. As the Bible warns: "You may be sure that your sin will find you out" (Numbers 32:23). Robert G. Lee, the late, great preacher of Bellevue Baptist Church in Memphis, preached about this truth in his memorable sermon on judgment entitled "Pay Day Someday."

In verse 12 Paul wrote, "All who sin apart from the law will also perish apart from the law, and all who sin under the law will be judged by the law." "The law" here refers to the Ten Commandments and other laws of God found in the Old Testament.

Ecclesiastes 12:14 says, "For God will bring every deed into judgment, including every hidden thing, whether it is good or evil." Jesus said that "men will have to give account on the day of judgment for every careless word they have spoken" (Matthew 12:36). Perhaps the toughest part of God's judgment has to do with what we did not do or say that we should have done or said.

Pastor William C. Duckworth has offered this modern parable of God's judgment: "For when I was hungry, you were obese. I was thirsty, and you were watering your lawn. I was a stranger, and you called the police and had me taken away. I was naked while you were saying, 'I must buy some new clothes. I just don't have a thing to wear.' I was ill, and you asked, 'Is it contagious?' I was in prison and you said, 'That's where your kind belongs.' "

Nobody gets away with anything. Neither O. J. Simpson, nor President Clinton, nor Saddam Hussein, nor you, nor me. Some judgment is immediate; some is delayed; and the rest will be waiting on us at the door to eternity.

In the Final Judgment, God Will Be Fair

Verses 13 through 15 of this second chapter of Romans are really one parenthetical statement by Paul about how God will judge. Although God will not play favorites, his judgment will be very discriminating. God will take into account one's limitations and opportunities. The Jews who had the benefit of Old Testament law will be held to a higher standard than those Gentiles who were never taught the law. By implication, we who were reared in the church will face a higher standard than someone who grew up in a land where the gospel is rarely, or never, heard.

From time to time, all of us are asked this age-old question: "How can God condemn the person who lives in a remote section of the Amazon Basin and has never heard of Jesus?" The answer is found here in chapter 2. God is wise enough to make allowances for everybody's special circumstances. No, God does not share all of his judgment criteria with us; if he did, our puny brains would be too small to take it in. But we can trust that God in his judgment will be fair.

Paul also points out that God will consider both our deeds and the motivation behind them. Verse 15 makes this clear. The father who steals because it seems the only way to provide food for his starving children may be worthy of leniency in God's eyes. On the other hand, if a person's real reason for giving $5,000 to a charity is to reap some political or business benefit, that will look rather shabby in God's view. God sees both deed and motivation.

The late Senator Sam Ervin of North Carolina used to tell about an experience he had in high school. One of his teachers required that each student answer the roll call each day with a quotation from the Bible. One day when Sam's name was called, he stood and with a big smile quoted Psalm 119, verse 99, which says, "I have more insight than all my teachers." The rest of the class laughed heartily, but the teacher was not pleased. She made Sam stay after school and memorize a lengthy poem. When he protested that the verse he had quoted was indeed in the Bible, she replied that he must still be punished because he did not quote it with reverence. Like that teacher, God will consider not only what we have done and said, but also the spirit in which we did or said it.

The Christ of Calvary Will Preside Over the Final Judgment

Note verse 16: "This will take place on the day when God will judge men's secrets through Jesus Christ, as my gospel declares." The role of Jesus in that judgment is even more explicit in John 5:22: "The Father judges no one, but has entrusted all judgment to the Son." Jesus as judge! That's hard for us to visualize. We think of Jesus as the one who welcomed little children, the healer of the sick, and the Savior on the cross. But Jesus as judge? That seems almost contradictory.

Yet who could be more qualified to judge? He lived in our world and experienced our circumstances. He was the only person who ever met the righteous demands of God. The really wonderful news is that this Jesus who will judge everybody is full of grace. That word "grace" means undeserved love, unmerited favor. His grace does not cancel judgment; rather, it satisfies judgment for those who repent and believe in him.

Jesus does not say to us, "Your sin is no big thing. Just forget it." Oh no! He says instead, "Your sin was a huge thing! A damnable thing! Look at the cross and see what it cost!" Because of Calvary we have a choice. We can repent of that sin and trust that Jesus paid the penalty for it. Or we can disregard the cross and pay the penalty ourselves. It's up to each of us.

The cross still casts its glorious shadow across all the centuries, past and future, proclaiming the most significant choice of our lives. Jesus will be, for each of us, either a Savior or judge. He wants to be our Savior, but the choice is ours. If we don't claim him as Savior, he will be our judge.

The popularity of the movie *Titanic* shows how that awful tragedy of 1912 still grips our imaginations. Just suppose that the day before that ship departed from its British port, the captain had offered free rides around the harbor in the lifeboats, paddled by the ship's crew. I doubt that there would have been a dozen takers. Who wants to be paddled around a dirty seaport in a rowboat?

But a few nights later, in the frigid waters of the North Atlantic, those places in the lifeboats were priceless. As that great ship floundered, men offered great wads of money for a seat in those lifeboats. But those places were not for sale.

Today any person can find a safe place at the foot of the cross. It costs nothing, though it cost Christ everything. All that is required of us is a willingness to repent and trust in Jesus Christ as Savior and Lord.

But one dare not delay. This life can end in a flash, as quickly as a drive-by shooting. And if this life ends without your having claimed Christ as Savior, you will meet him as judge. Then not all the money on earth will be able to purchase safe passage for you.

Who will Jesus be for you—judge or Savior? The choice is yours.

CHAPTER ELEVEN

CLEANSED BY CHRIST

Revelation 7:9-17

On the Friday of a long Fourth of July weekend, a certain service station was backed up with customers. A local pastor had been waiting in line for some time. A service station attendant said to him, "Sorry for the delay, pastor. Seems like folks always wait until the last minute to get ready for a trip they know they're going on." The pastor smiled and replied, "Yeah, I have the same problem in my business."

All of us are going to spend eternity somewhere. There are only two possibilities. None of us knows his or her departure date. It amazes me that some intelligent people who would not dream of being unprepared for retirement make little or no preparation for their permanent, eternal destination.

Martin Marty, a religious historian, says, "Now the only time you hear of heaven is when somebody has died."[1] Yet Peter Kreeft, a professor of philosophy at Boston College, states that heaven "is the reason that God banged out the Big Bang 18 billion years ago. Next to the idea of God, the idea of heaven is the greatest idea that has ever entered into the heart of man, woman or child."[2]

Recently, an eight-year-old child wrote to Billy Graham and asked, "Where is Heaven? Do you think the astronauts will discover Heaven someday?" Graham wrote back and said, "No, the astronauts will never discover it as they explore space. . . . Heaven is not just a corner of the universe somewhere. . . . Heaven is of a different order, beyond the limits of our universe. The Bible says, 'No eye has seen, no ear has heard, no mind has conceived what God has prepared for those who love him' (1 Corinthians 2:9). You see, Heaven is the dwelling place of God. It is a place of perfection and peace."

The seventh chapter of the book of Revelation gives us a glimpse of heaven. A disciple named John, exiled on the island of Patmos, was given a vision of heaven. Let's look at what he tells us about heaven and how to get there.

Heaven Will Be a Cosmopolitan Place

Notice verse 9: "After this I looked and there before me was a great multitude that no one could count, from every nation, tribe, people and language, standing before the throne and in front of the Lamb." What an amazing diversity of people will be in heaven: rednecks and royalty, former prostitutes and politicians, former homosexuals and Hollywood stars—even some preachers will be there, though fewer than expected.

Some convicted murderers will be in heaven. I'm sure that Karla Faye Tucker will be there. Just moments before the state of Texas executed her in February 1998, she declared that she was going to be face-to-face with Jesus.

Just imagine! Worshiping side by side will be Southern Baptists, Episcopalians, and Pentecostals. In heaven, the Episcopalians won't mind if the Pentecostals raise their hands. And heaven will be overrun by children. Every single child, born and unborn, who died before reaching the age of discretion will be there. What laughter and joy will fill the place!

Between Here and Heaven, We Must Go Through Tribulation

In verse 14, these residents of heaven are referred to as those "who have come out of the great tribulation." That tribulation probably refers to the awful time of suffering that Jesus predicted in Matthew 13 and 24, the hard times before Jesus returns in triumph. But isn't it a fact that all Christians must pass through some tribulation and trouble as they journey with Christ? Jesus said, "Blessed are you when people insult you, persecute you and falsely say all kinds of evil against you because of me. Rejoice and be glad, because great is your reward in heaven" (Matthew 5:11-12).

If you stand up for Christ and his Holy Word, you will be persecuted. But that shouldn't surprise us. Look what the world did to Paul! Look what the world did to our Lord and Savior! Are we better than they? Since when did the costs of discipleship go into recession?

In addition to the flak we take for standing up for truth, life seems to parcel out some trouble to every person rather indiscriminately. For many people in my age bracket, the late Roy Rogers was our cowboy hero when we were children. Roy Rogers and his wife, Dale Evans, were a devoted Christian couple who were unashamed to stand up for Christ. They had nine children, several of them adopted. That family, though devoutly Christian, was not spared from tragedy. Daughter Robin was mentally retarded and died before her second birthday. Korean-born Debbie was killed in a church bus accident. The following year their son John choked to death. Roy and Dale understood that Christians are not immune to heartbreak in this world. Remember Jesus' promise: "In this world you will have trouble. But take heart! I have overcome the world" (John 16:33).

All Residents of Heaven
Will Have Washed Their Robes
in the Blood of the Lamb

In ancient Old Testament times, lambs were sacrificed at the temple for the sins of the people. God intended that practice to prepare humanity to understand the mission of Jesus, the Messiah. The life, death, and resurrection of Jesus made such animal sacrifices unnecessary. Jesus offered himself as the sacrificial Lamb of God. His death on the cross was the perfect and sufficient sacrifice, once and for all time, for the sin of the world. Believers who place their personal trust in Jesus' sacrifice are the ones who, in the words of Revelation, have "washed their robes . . . in the blood of the Lamb" (v. 14).

When I was a boy growing up in Methodist churches, we sang an old hymn that had these words:

> Have you been to Jesus for the cleansing power?
> Are you washed in the blood of the Lamb?
> Are you fully trusting in his grace this hour?
> Are you washed in the blood of the Lamb?

The modern mind doesn't know how to relate to this talk of blood. In fact, the sight of blood causes some people to pass out. You don't hear much talk about the blood of Jesus in "nice respectable churches," and you won't find the hymn I just mentioned in many modern hymnals.

The Bible says a lot about the shed blood of Jesus. You can find it in places like 1 John 1:7: "But if we walk in the light . . . the blood of Jesus, his Son, purifies us from all sin." You can find it in 1 Peter 1:18-19: "For you know that it was not with perishable things such as silver or gold that you were redeemed from the empty way of life handed down to you from your forefathers, but with the precious blood of Christ, a lamb without blemish or defect." And then there is that powerful verse from

Hebrews that says "without the shedding of blood there is no forgiveness" (9:22).

How are we moderns to understand all this talk of blood? Remember, God built this world on a moral foundation. Sin is a violation of God's order. Because God is just and altogether righteous, he cannot ignore or wink at sin. To do so would be to deny his very nature. Somebody always pays for sin. No one but Jesus was good enough and great enough to pay for the sins of the whole world, and it cost him his life.

Let me illustrate. Suppose a man is driving his car through a residential area at night. The posted speed limit is 35 miles per hour. But this man is in a hurry. He has been to a happy hour party, had three drinks, and stayed too long. He is driving 60 miles per hour. A seven-year-old child is playing outdoors on this warm summer evening. She darts into the street from behind a parked car. The man tries to stop but it's too late. He looks down on the broken body of the little girl, and frantically calls 911 on his car phone.

Later, the driver is pacing up and down outside the hospital's emergency room. The child's father comes rushing in. He was out of town when he got word, and rushed back as quickly as possible. About that time, the doctor comes out and tells this sad group that though the child is going to live, she may have suffered permanent brain damage. Then the driver, with liquor still on his breath, says to the parents, "Oh, please forgive me."

There is no way in the world that those parents could quickly or easily respond, "Oh sure, we forgive you." An easy forgiveness would trivialize the awful wrong done to the little girl. If and when those parents are able to forgive that driver, it will be on the other side of tears, anguish, and a broken heart. Truly, those parents would be wounded for the driver's transgression.

All of us are like that driver. God is like those parents. Do you see why real grace is never cheap? Real forgiveness always costs the forgiver. It caused Jesus, who knew no sin, to become sin for us, so that we might stand before God one day, covered by his righteousness. If you repent of sin and believe Jesus died for you, you have been washed in the blood of the Lamb.

Allow me to summarize the message of the whole Bible in four brief statements. All the rest is prologue or follow-through. Here is the essence of God's message to us in the Bible:

(1) I love you as you are, sin and all.
(2) You have a sin problem, a deadly spiritual virus, that if left untreated will wreck your life and separate you from me forever.
(3) Through the cross, I have provided the only cure for your sin problem.
(4) That cure, called "salvation," is yours if you repent of sin and claim Jesus Christ by faith as your Savior and Lord.

Philip Yancey, in his wonderful book entitled *What's So Amazing About Grace?*, refers to the movie *The Last Emperor*. In that movie, the young child who is the last emperor of China has a thousand eunuchs to serve him. His brother asked him, "What happens when you do wrong?" The boy replied, "When I do wrong, someone else is punished." The brother watched as the emperor broke a jar and one of the servants received a beating for it.

Note this! As Yancey says, Jesus reversed this pattern: "when the servants erred, the King was punished."[3] When you and I found ourselves hopelessly mired in sin, the king of kings, Jesus Christ, bore our guilt and suffered our penalty. If you repent of sin and claim Jesus

Christ as your personal Savior and Lord, then one day you will stand with all the saints in heaven, covered by the spotless clothing of your Lord.

Have you been washed in the blood of the Lamb? It can happen today!

NOTES

1. David Van Biema, "Does Heaven Exist?" *Time,* March 24, 1997, p. 73.

2. Ibid., p. 72.

3. Philip Yancey, *What's So Amazing About Grace?* (Grand Rapids: Zondervan Publishing House, 1997), p. 60.

CHAPTER TWELVE

THE WITNESS OF THE SPIRIT

Romans 8:9-17

Just south of the town of Bolivar, Tennessee, is the grave of Colonel Ezekiel Polk, grandfather of President James K. Polk. He died around 1815. He composed his own epitaph to appear on his gravestone. It was a kind of poetic commentary on the times. In it he took a pot-shot at the Methodists, whose enthusiasm he did not appreciate. He wrote: "Methodists with their camp bawling, will be the cause of our down falling."

Often at Methodist camp meetings or revivals, people would start bawling with tears of joy. It had to do with the doctrine of Christian assurance, or the witness of the Spirit. Methodists have always preached that if one repents of sin and trusts in Jesus Christ as Savior and Lord, one can actually know that one has been saved, born again, and reconciled to God. One doesn't have to just hope that one is saved—one can know!

The key biblical reference for this doctrine is Romans 8:15, 16: "And by him we cry, '*Abba*, Father.' The Spirit himself testifies with our spirit that we are God's children." The late great bishop and seminary dean, William R. Cannon, referred to this as "Methodism's most distinctive doctrinal characteristic."[1]

I think back forty-five years to that blessed evening, when in a tiny rural church I first experienced salvation; I had the assurance of the Spirit that very evening. I can recall riding home with my father and sister. Though I was not theologically literate enough to explain what had happened, I knew I was different. I knew Christ had accepted me and that I belonged to him. That assurance has never left me.

This assurance is more than a feeling. Its authenticity is not measured in emotion. It remains even when feelings are low and troubles are as thick as mosquitoes in the Mississippi Delta. This sense of assurance has nothing whatsoever to do with the New Age flakiness you hear about on television, such as channeling, imagining, and psychic intuition.

Paul taught us that two witnesses are involved, that of the Holy Spirit and then our own. The Holy Spirit's witness is primary. Our spirit is the echo. When the two agree, our soul reverberates with joy. To what shall I compare this experience? Have you ever sat in the moonlight and told your beloved for the first time that you love her? And then you held your breath because you couldn't be exactly sure what her response would be. How relieved you were when she whispered back, "I love you too." Didn't that feel good? The witness of the Spirit is even better. That's when God's Spirit whispers to us, "You are an adopted member of God's family," and our spirit responds, "I sure am, and it feels wonderful."

The founder of Methodism, John Wesley, offered this definition of the witness of the Spirit: it is "an inward impression on the soul, whereby the Spirit of God directly 'witnesses to my spirit that I am a child of God'; that Jesus Christ hath loved me, and given himself for me; that all my sins are blotted out, and I, even I, am reconciled to God."[2] Wesley said of this doctrine, "It is one grand part of the testimony which God has given [Methodists] to bear to all mankind."[3]

How sure can we be of our salvation? John Wesley said that God's Spirit gives the believer such an assurance of adoption that "he can no more doubt the reality" of it "than he can doubt the shining of the sun while he stands in the full blaze of his beams."[4] That's pretty solid confidence! Are you that sure of your salvation? Are you certain that if you departed this world tonight, you would be bound for heaven?

God wants us all to be sure of our salvation. In 1 John 5:13 we read, "I write these things to you who believe in the name of the Son of God so that you may know that you have eternal life." God's Word assures it, and the Spirit confirms it.

The Witness of the Spirit Gives Us an Intimacy with God

We can call God "Daddy"! That's what the Aramaic word "*Abba*" means. That is the term Jesus used to address God in prayer. We believers don't have to refer to God as "Your Highness" or "Your Holiness." We may call him "Daddy" because we have been adopted into his family.

I love the story of two little first-grade boys who were brothers. On the first day of school, the children were introducing themselves. One of the boys said, "Me and Jack are brothers. One of us is adopted and one is not, but I can't remember which is which."

Well, we Christians don't have to worry about that. All of us believers are adopted. God nominates us to be members of his family. When we respond in faith and God grants us a new birth, the adoption happens. Then the Spirit confirms that it's a "done deal."

The Witness of the Spirit Gives Us Courage and Confidence

Paul in verse 15 of Romans 8 noted that "you did not receive a spirit that makes you a slave again to fear." In a letter to his young assistant, Timothy, Paul said something similar: "God did not give us a spirit of timidity, but a spirit of power, of love and of self-discipline" (2 Timothy 1:7).

Many a good person has failed because he or she had a wishbone where a backbone should have been. The Holy Spirit gives us backbone. The Holy Spirit reminds us that we "can do everything through him who gives [us] strength" (Philippians 4:13).

The Witness of the Spirit Gives Us a Sure Hope for the Future

Through Christian assurance we know that we are "heirs of God and co-heirs with Christ" (Romans 8:17). Back during the worst part of the Great Depression, a distraught woman walked into the office of a major insurance company. She did not understand how life insurance worked. Very sadly, she said to the clerk, "I'm afraid I can't continue to pay the premiums on my husband's life insurance policy. He has been dead for six months now, and I just can't afford it."

The amazed clerk called the office manager. He looked over the policy and then almost caused the woman to faint when he told her that she would soon receive a check for $200,000. She thought she was poor when actually she was wealthy.

Now let me apply that story to the spiritual realm. All the spiritual riches that belong to Jesus Christ—his salvation, his power, his joy, and his peace—belong to us, too. He paid the premiums on Calvary's cross. All the benefits are ours if we just endorse the policy through faith.

But you might say, "I don't have that assurance. How can I get it?" You would not be alone. One survey says that at least 90 percent of all Christians in America are leading defeated lives. I am convinced that the witness of the Spirit can transform that defeat into victory.

If you do not have the assurance of salvation and adoption as a child of God, ask God for it daily. Keep on asking until you receive. Remember Jesus' promise: "If you then, though you are evil, know how to give good gifts to your children, how much more will your Father in heaven give the Holy Spirit to those who ask him!" (Luke 11:13).

The Holy Spirit confirms the truth of one's salvation and adoption. That is the witness of the Spirit. Once you receive the witness, tell people regularly why you are so joyful!

I love the story that is told about an Easterner who walked into a Western saloon one day. He was amazed to see a dog sitting at a table playing poker with three men. He asked someone, "Can that dog really read cards?" "Yeah," said one of the men. "But he ain't much of a player. Whenever he gets a good hand, he wags his tail." Because of the grace of God, we are holding the best hand on earth. Our joy ought to show!

Let's suppose that you were unable to have a child the natural way. But because of your great desire to love and raise a child, you decided to go through the complicated process of adoption. Let's suppose that after a year of much work, prayer, and considerable expense, a precious little six-day-old girl was placed in your arms.

Even before you gazed upon her for the first time, you anticipated that one day you would share with her the fact that she is adopted. Sure enough, the day came when she was old enough to understand. You took her on your lap and said something like this: "Honey, you did not come to us the way most children do. They are born into a certain family whether that family wants them or not, whether that family can take care of them or not. But that's not how you came to us. We dreamed about you and prayed for you for years before you came to us. We yearned for you. We thought our hearts would break if God did not send you to us. Then, on a wonderful day we will never forget, a phone call brought the great news. Someone told us that you had been born. Your mother was not able to take care of you, but she loved you so much that she made sure you had the best parents that could be found. Six days later you were placed in our arms, and we cried tears of joy. We adopted you. Everything we have will be yours one day. It would be impossible for us to love you any more even if you had been born into our family. Do you understand?"

That's the kind of conversation you would have with your daughter. Why? Because you would want her to feel absolutely secure in your family. If you as human parents want your child to feel good and secure about adoption, don't you think that the heavenly Father is even more determined that our status in his family be solid and secure? Doesn't it make sense that his Spirit would bear witness with our spirit that we are God's children?

NOTES

1. Quoted in Lovett H. Weems, Jr., *Pocket Guide to John Wesley's Message Today* (Nashville: Abingdon Press, 1991), p. 34.

2. John Wesley, *The Works of John Wesley Vol. 1: Sermons I (1-33)*, ed. by Albert C. Outler (Nashville: Abingdon Press, 1984), p. 274.

3. Ibid., p. 285.

4. Ibid., p. 276.

CHAPTER THIRTEEN

IF YOU'RE A DECENT PERSON, IS THAT ENOUGH?

Acts 2:36-39, Romans 10:9-10

When baseball season rolls around, I begin to pay attention to the Atlanta Braves. I enjoy watching them play baseball, and some nights I really wish they would. Baseball lost one of its great personalities when Harry Caray died in 1998. Harry was more than just the voice of the Chicago Cubs. He was a beloved institution in the Windy City. Though his singing voice was less than spectacular, no game in Chicago was complete without hearing Harry lead the fans in a rousing, seventh-inning version of "Take Me Out to the Ballgame."

Harry wrote a book shortly before he died. It was titled, appropriately, *Holy Cow!* That title reminded everybody of Harry's customary way of describing a home run. He would say, "It might be—it could be—It is! Holy cow!" In his book Harry wrote as follows: "I am not a religious man. I've made some mistakes in life. Dutchie is my third wife . . . and I've paid a lot of alimony in my time. But I've always believed in the Almighty God. I've always believed that if you live your life as a decent person, the umpire in the end will say you did it right."[1]

Harry's theology is perhaps the most popular version in America. Don't most people believe that if you affirm the existence of God and try to be decent, God will grade on the curve and you'll slide on into heaven?

Professor Leander E. Keck of Yale Divinity School has observed that "far too much theology today underwrites a striver's manual instead of a gift certificate from the God who, in Paul's words, justifies the ungodly (Romans 4:5)."[2]

Far be it from me to judge the eternal destiny of Harry Caray or anyone else, but his theology is less than Christian. Even the devil believes that God exists. And the Bible does not say that being decent is enough to please God. Let's invite the Bible to answer our question: What is required of us in order to be absolutely confident that we are saved and on the way to heaven?

Our text, Acts 2:36-39, is the hard-hitting climax of Simon Peter's great Pentecost sermon. What a sermon it was! When he extended the invitation, three thousand people came forward and were baptized. In verse 36, Simon Peter combines a stinging indictment with a ringing affirmation: "God has made this Jesus, whom you crucified, both Lord and Christ."

While the message of the gospel is a joyful reminder about the awesome love of God, it is also a humbling reprimand. Each of us is a sinner and if we get what we deserve, we will go straight to hell.

God is utterly righteous and pure. He cannot abide sin. Yet all of us, just because of sinful thoughts, are knee-deep in sin by nine o'clock each morning. This morning's newspaper is sufficient to stimulate within us a sinful train of hateful, lustful, racist, and greedy thoughts.

Notice that Simon Peter accused his hearers of having crucified Jesus. Yet in all probability, none of them was in the mob that shouted "Crucify him!" Certainly none helped the Roman soldiers pound iron spikes through his flesh. Nevertheless, Simon Peter called them guilty. We are guilty, too. My sin made it necessary for Jesus to agonize for six hours on that splintery cross. Our sin thrust a spear into his holy side as surely as that Roman soldier did.

Verse 37 tells us that Simon Peter's listeners were convicted of their role in Jesus' crucifixion. Nobody argued with Simon Peter or tried to blame the Roman soldiers or the High Priest. Instead, they interrupted Simon Peter, asking, "What shall we do?"

Notice Simon Peter's reply in verse 38. He did not say, "Try to behave yourself better." He did not say, "Be more careful to tithe your income." He did not say, "Attend temple worship more regularly." He did not say, "Give more money to the poor." Though all of those things are commendable, none will save your soul.

First, said Simon Peter, "Repent." That means to admit that we have failed to measure up to God's expectations. We are sinners. We have a spiritual virus that has no earthly cure. To repent means far more than just saying, "I'm sorry." It also means to decide to live differently with God's help. Not only that, true repentance causes one to make amends if possible.

A few months ago, I received the following letter of repentance from an anonymous, out-of-town source:

Dear Pastor,
 Several years ago I lived in Memphis and periodically visited your church. During this period I suffered from a drug and alcohol problem. I am now in Alcoholics Anonymous and have been in recovery for almost five years. Part of the healing process for me is to go back over my past and make amends for wrongs done to others. My best recollection is that I gave the church two bad checks for about $50 each. I am enclosing a cashier's check for $100 to cover the church's loss. The people of Christ Methodist were always loving and certainly did their best to help me; unfortunately, I was beyond human aid. I will always think of your church with fond memories. What I did was wrong. I hope you will accept this check and my apology. May God continue to bless all of you.

That is repentance: confessing one's error, going in a different direction, and trying to make amends.

Simon Peter's second command was to "be baptized, every one of you, in the name of Jesus Christ for the forgiveness of your sins" (Acts 2:38). This statement must have shocked his hearers because this man Jesus had recently been executed as a blasphemer and heretic. Now Simon Peter was declaring him to be the Messiah, the Son of God!

What must we believe about Jesus in order to be saved? Notice that in verse 38, Simon Peter connected Jesus directly to the forgiveness of sins. That's important. It means that it is not enough to believe that Jesus was God's Son. Even the devil knows that. It is not enough to agree with some of his teaching. Many intelligent people do.

The crucial matter is to believe that Jesus came to this earth on a love mission to reach you in particular. When he died on that cross, he was paying the penalty for your sin, providing the only way by which you could be freed from evil and prepared to spend eternity with God. My name and yours were written on the cross of Christ.

If you believe that and are filled with gratitude for that sacrifice, you will naturally want the living Christ-Spirit to be the leader of your life. At the moment when you extend that invitation, Jesus starts a personal relationship with you. At that moment you are saved.

In verse 38, Simon Peter urges all believers to be baptized. Baptism is a public declaration that Jesus is Lord. Baptism is not the same as being saved. A thief who died on a cross beside Jesus was saved without baptism. Baptism is normally the next step after having received the gift of salvation. When we allow the water of baptism to be applied to us, God's Holy Spirit seals and strengthens us in our relationship with Christ.

Baptism is a way of going public for Christ. Remember these words of Paul: "If you confess with your mouth, 'Jesus is Lord,' and believe in your heart that God raised him from the dead, you will be saved. For it is with your heart that you believe and are justified, and it is with your mouth that you confess and are saved" (Romans 10:9-10).

In the latter part of verse 38, Simon Peter tells the people that, in addition to salvation, they will receive the gift of the Holy Spirit. In that very moment when we trust in Jesus Christ as forgiver and leader, the Holy Spirit takes up residence in our hearts and minds. The Holy Spirit gives us an assurance that we are eternally saved and adopted as children of God. The Holy Spirit provides power and discernment for victorious living. The Holy Spirit leads us deeper into the truth of Christ. And, as icing on the cake, the Holy Spirit plants a little bit of heaven in our souls in the form of inner peace and abiding joy. We have a great and generous God!

Where do you stand today? Are you just a decent person who hopes that someday God will grade on the curve? Do you pay lip service to Jesus Christ but know deep in your heart that he is not the leader of your life?

You can change all that today. In verse 39, Simon Peter declares that this offer of abundant and eternal life in Jesus Christ is "for you and your children and for all who are far off—for all whom the Lord our God will call." Maybe God is calling you today.

The extremely successful football coach at Florida State University, Bobby Bowden, often relates the following true story from the world of baseball. Back in the 1920s, the Washington Senators had a great player named Leon Allen Gosling. As you might expect, he was nicknamed "Goose." The Senators played in the 1924 World Series. In the seventh and deciding game, Goose came to the plate in the bottom of the ninth inning with the score tied. He got just the pitch he wanted. He slammed a hard line drive just over the glove of the shortstop. It rolled all the way to the fence. Goose rounded first base and fixed his eye on the outfielder making the play. The outfielder bobbled the ball just for a moment. That was all Goose needed. He turned on the speed, rounded second base, and headed for third. His eyes were on the third base coach, who had a hard call to make. Finally, at the last moment, he signaled Goose to head for home. The ball reached the catcher just a half-second before Goose did. Goose did exactly as he had been trained to do. He hit the catcher as hard as he could, knocking him six feet backwards. The ball squirted out of his hand, and Goose touched home plate.

The huge crowd went wild. Thousands of fans poured out onto the field. In such chaos and confusion, no one noticed the first baseman retrieving the ball. The first baseman quickly conferred with the umpire and the pitcher. When order was restored, the pitcher flipped the ball to the first baseman who then tagged first base. The first baseman appealed to the umpire, claiming that Goose had never touched first base. The umpire upheld the appeal and declared Goose to be out.

Some people sail through life like Goose running the bases. They seem to get all the breaks. They are prosperous and healthy. Everything they touch seems to turn to gold. But if, in the process of living, one never repents and trusts in Jesus Christ as forgiver and leader, one never makes it to first base. One day the umpire of heaven and earth will declare, "You are out!"

At such a time it will not help one iota to declare, "But Lord, I was a decent person, far more decent than most." The only people who will make it home to heaven will be those who have repented of sin and have trusted in Jesus Christ as Savior and Lord.

Perhaps you have heard the gospel preached many times but have never actually responded to it. I want to give you a chance to change that. I'm going to offer a prayer of commitment and invite you to pray this prayer with me. If you pray this prayer sincerely, you will be responding in faith to the grace offered in Jesus Christ. God will hear and respond, saving your soul and transforming your life.

Let us pray: "Dear Lord Jesus, I know that I am a sinner and need your forgiveness. I believe that you died for my sins. I want to turn from my sins and become a new person. I now invite you to come into my heart and life. I trust in you as my Savior and pledge to follow you as my Lord. Amen."

NOTES

1. Harry Caray, *Holy Cow!* (New York: Villard Books, 1989), p. 16.
2. Leander E. Keck, *The Church Confident* (Nashville: Abingdon Press, 1993), p. 56.

CHAPTER FOURTEEN

DOES TRUTH HAVE MANY VERSIONS?

John 8:31-32, 18:33-38

When I was a youngster of about twelve, I had a summer job at a service station. The young fellow who worked in the grease pit often sang country and gospel melodies. I remember the words of one of his songs: "That word 'broad-minded' is spelled S-I-N,/I read it in my Bible; Thou shalt not enter in."

How times have changed since the 1950s! To refer to someone today as being "broad-minded" is a high compliment. Tolerance is seen as one of the highest virtues. The hot-button term in our culture is "exclusive." "Narrow-minded" people are regarded as the enemies of tolerance, openness, and freedom.

In America, we believe in religious toleration. You can even be a Satan-worshiper and have your religious freedom respected. But along with our toleration has come the dangerous idea that no religion has exclusive claims to truth. R. C. Sproul says that making exclusive religious claims in America is "like attacking baseball, hot dogs, motherhood, and apple pie (not to mention Chevrolet)."[1]

Much of the public believes that there is no such thing as absolute truth. In their view, whatever works for you is truth. Truth is not so much discovered as it is invented. Many young adults say, "Don't impose your values on me; let me determine what is right or wrong for me."

Tolerance is a beautiful virtue if it means respecting someone's right to disagree or to be different. But for many, tolerance means something very dangerous—that all values, beliefs, lifestyles, and claims to truth are equal.

God's Word, the Bible, does not talk about versions of truth, degrees of truth, or shades of truth. It talks about the truth. Jesus said, "I am the way and the truth and the life" (John 14:6). Again, Jesus said that "you will know the truth, and the truth will set you free" (John 8:32). The most scandalous thing about Christianity is its claim to represent absolute truth. Let's examine this matter further as we look at our scripture, John 18:33-38.

Let me remind you of the setting. On a Thursday night, Jewish leaders and their armed guards arrested Jesus. He was taken to the home of the high priest. For most of that night he was ridiculed, beaten, and interrogated. Very early the next morning, he was taken to the Praetorium, a remodeled castle that was the residence of the Roman governor, Pontius Pilate. The Jewish leaders brought Jesus to Pilate because he alone could impose the death penalty.

Pilate did not want to have Jesus executed, but he was even less eager to upset relations with the Jewish establishment. Pilate already had a few negative reports in his file back in Rome. Another one could jeopardize his career advancement. Pilate asked Jesus, "Are you the king of the Jews?"—wondering if Jesus was the leader of some conspiracy. "Is that your own idea," Jesus asked, "or did others talk to you about me?"

Pilate probably cursed at that point, irritated that this man who should have been on his knees begging for mercy would dare to question him. Jesus wanted to know if there was a glimmer of faith in Pilate. Imagine that! Jesus cared about the salvation of the man about to sentence him to death.

Jesus went on to explain, "My kingdom is not of this world. If it were, my servants would fight to prevent my arrest by the Jews. But now my kingdom is from another place." "You are a king, then!" Pilate said. Jesus replied, "You are right in saying I am a king. . . . for this I came into the world, to testify to the truth." With cynical disgust, Pilate snorted, "What is truth?" and walked away. Pilate believed that truth was whatever Caesar declared it to be, because his military legions could back up his truth. According to Pilate, truth without power is nothing.

But Jesus declared that truth is ordained by God. It is not subject to popular vote. It is eternal and unchanging. Jesus himself is the ultimate expression of truth. The Bible, God's inspired Word, is our true rule and guide for faith and ethics. To make such a claim is to invite questions and debate. Let me ask and try to answer some inevitable questions.

Don't All Religions Teach the Same Thing?

No, they do not. R. C. Sproul explains the uniqueness of Christianity as follows: "The Christian claim is that in the person of Jesus of Nazareth we meet God incarnate. Buddha never claimed to be anything more than a man. Mohammed claimed nothing more than to be a prophet. Moses and Confucius were mortals. If Christ was in fact God incarnate, then it is a travesty of justice to ascribe equal honor to Him and to the others."[2]

As Long as Each Person Is Genuinely Sincere, What Difference Does It Make What He or She Believes?

It makes a difference because one can be sincerely wrong. I'm sure that the followers of Jim Jones were sincere when they followed him to Guyana in the late

1970s, but they were sincerely wrong and it cost them their lives. The next time you get stopped for going 55 in a 40 mile-per-hour zone, try telling the police officer how sincere you were in your belief that the speed limit was 55. Note how impressed the officer is.

Some religious people refuse to take any of the medicines that God has graciously allowed us to discover and use for our health. These folks suffer needlessly and sometimes die for their beliefs. They are sincere, no doubt, but wrong.

Is It Narrow-minded for Christians to Think Their Faith Is Right and Other Religions Are Wrong?

It is not narrow-minded if Christians have examined the evidence and have found Christianity trustworthy in ways that other religions are not. Let's consider the evidence.

First, detailed predictions about Jesus were written hundreds of years before he was born. Jesus fulfilled every single prediction. One of those prophecies told what town he would be born in and where he would be raised. Isaiah 53:5 stated that he would be "pierced for our transgressions." This was written hundreds of years before crucifixion was invented as a means of execution.

Second, Jesus performed miracles in broad daylight, in front of both his supporters and his detractors. So compelling was the evidence that none of his opponents challenged whether the miracles had actually occurred.

A third consideration is this: Jesus' greatest miracle—his own resurrection from the dead—was so compelling that his disciples, without exception, allowed themselves to be executed when a simple denial of the resurrection would have saved their lives. If Jesus had not risen from the dead, his enemies would have quickly produced his body. But they couldn't, because there was no body to be found.

This does not mean that we should be disrespectful toward other religions. We will never have a chance to share the gospel with Muslim, Hindu, or Jewish people unless we treat them respectfully. It is never proper for us to judge those who believe in other religions. Only God is capable of doing that properly, with justice and mercy. But neither should we ever embrace the cultural myth that all religions are equally true.

R. C. Sproul asks:

> How can Buddhism be true when it *denies* the existence of a personal God and at the same time Christianity be true when it *affirms* the existence of a personal God? . . . Can Orthodox Judaism be right when it denies life after death and Christianity be equally right when it affirms life after death? Can classical Islam have a valid ethic that endorses the killing of infidels while at the same time the Christian ethic of loving your enemies be equally valid?[3]

The late Bishop William R. Cannon insisted that Christians must share the gospel with persons of other faiths.

> Everybody outside the church is fair game for the church to evangelize, and in turn to win for Jesus Christ. Even in dialoque with persons of other religions there is always the hope, nay more than that, the expectation that they will in the course of honest discussion see the supremacy of Christianity to their own faith because of Jesus Christ, and capitulate to him by believing and accepting his gospel. This is what is happening in Asia and Africa. . . . This is what can and should happen everywhere.[4]

Doesn't it seem strange to you that whereas some people doubt that the truth can be known in spiritual matters, they don't feel that way about other sectors of life? You expect absolute, precise truth when your accountant is figuring your taxes or when your physician is diagnosing your health problem. Why do many people assume that absolute truth can be known in most areas of life except in the spiritual realm?

Last summer while on vacation, I got into my car one day and discovered that it would not start. I called AAA and soon a mechanic arrived. He said, "It's either the battery or the starter. I'll have to run some tests to determine which one." But he did not say, "Mr. Bouknight, it's one or the other. Take your choice. As long as you believe sincerely that your choice is correct, your diagnosis will be fine." That mechanic was narrow-minded enough to believe that he could discern the truth about my car.

God never said in his Word that all roads lead to him. In fact, his Word declares just the opposite. Jesus said, "Enter through the narrow gate. For wide is the gate and broad is the road that leads to destruction, and many enter through it. But small is the gate and narrow the road that leads to life, and only a few find it" (Matthew 7:13-14).

Well then, maybe it's not Christians who are narrow-minded; maybe it's God. After all, Jesus himself said, "I am the way and the truth and the life. No one comes to the Father except through me." Now, that sounds mighty narrow-minded and exclusive. Why would God be that way?

Let's suppose that there is a righteous and holy God. He created a man and a woman, Adam and Eve, to fellowship with him, and placed only one limitation on them. He told them not to eat the fruit of one particular tree in a garden full of fruit-bearing trees. But Adam and Eve promptly violated the rule. Adam blamed it on his wife, setting a terrible precedent that has persisted to this day.

In the centuries that followed, the descendants of Adam and Eve did everything imaginable to offend our holy and righteous God. Nevertheless, God kept sending them messenger after messenger to remind them of his love and to recall them to him. Most of these messengers were abused and persecuted; some were killed.

Finally, in a desperate act of grace, God himself visited this planet as a man named Jesus. However, instead of being welcomed, this Jesus was slandered, mocked, tortured, and murdered. Yet, miraculously, God did not wipe out humanity in a fit of revenge and start a new human race in a different solar system. Instead, God accepted the murder of his only Son as the atoning sacrifice for the sins of the very people who murdered him. In fact, God offered to his Son's murderers and their descendants total amnesty, complete forgiveness, and eternal salvation.

Suppose God did all this and then said to the human race, "I ask only one thing of you—that you admit your sin and honor and worship my Son alone." Supposing God did all that, would you have the unmitigated gall to say, "Lord, you are mighty narrow-minded not to offer several ways of salvation rather than just one"?

Several years ago, at an international Christian conference, a speaker made the following statement: "Christianity is just one of several world religions. We must not presume that Christianity is better or more distinctive than the rest." Seated in that assembly was a Protestant church leader from a country where, even today, Christians are often imprisoned or killed for their faith. They live in a hostile Muslim environment. When the speaker had finished, this leader stood and asked to speak. He said, "If the speaker we just heard is correct, I must leave this conference at once and return to my country and inform my people that it is no longer necessary for them to die for the name of Jesus." There was silence in that great auditorium as delegates remembered the thousands of saints, including most of the original disciples, who gave their lives rather than deny that Jesus is "the way and the truth and the life."

According to the Bible, the truth is narrow. Beware of that word "broad-minded." It may be spelled "S-I-N."

NOTES

1. R. C. Sproul, *Reason to Believe* (Grand Rapids: Zondervan, 1982), p. 36.

2. Ibid., p. 43.

3. Ibid., p. 36.

4. William R. Cannon, *A Magnificent Obsession* (Nashville: Abingdon Press, 1999), p. 357.